Bark Until Heard

Among the Silenced Dogs, I Found My Voice

Becky Monroe

ISBN: 1507841248
ISBN: 9781507841242

Cover design by Steven Novak
Cover photo by Becky Monroe
Author photo by Tom Maple

For #171

My very existence changed the day I met you.

*I will forever be grateful for our fateful encounter
and for allowing myself to follow my heart
and find my voice.*

There would be no story without you.

PREFACE

There is a picture of me . . . my face is red and blotchy and giant tears are streaming down. It was taken on my second birthday. My mom thought it would be fun to have a piñata. As the birthday girl, I was given the bat first. Before I could get blindfolded, I looked up at what I was supposed to hit and started to cry. "I don't want to hurt the donkey," I said. Hysterical, I watched each of my birthday guests whack at the stuffed piñata. And when it broke and the candy came crashing to the ground, I looked away. My mom has shared that story with me many times. Even at the age of two, I knew hurting an animal wasn't worth what you could get out of it.

Forty years later, that picture still makes my heart sink. There are some things you are just born with, and mine was an unbridled compassion for animals. I couldn't have been more blessed because knowing an animal's unconditional love is the most amazing gift of all. I wish everyone could experience it.

The Box (A Puppy-Mill Story)
Copyright © 2008 by Chuck Wegner

I was born in a box, a "birthing box," they called it. My brothers and sisters were all around me and, of course, Mom was there too. She tended to our needs, kept us warm and fed, and she tried her best to keep us clean. We had a little "sun" in the top of our box, and sometimes it would go dark and then it got colder. I didn't like that, but my family was all around me, so I managed.

As the weeks went by I grew a little, and every once in a while a giant would come and open the small door to our box. I caught the scent of fear from Mom each time that door opened. I didn't know what the giant wanted, but I knew that Mom was scared of him, so I was too. Then one day the giant opened the door and reached a long arm in to pick up one of my brothers. He squealed and whined and tried to hide, but the giant's hand caught him and held him up. The giant said, "I'm gonna keep this one, he's worth a lot more cuz he's so small." I was glad I was growing every day because I didn't want to be the littlest one, but I wondered: If the giant was going to keep my little brother, what was going to happen to the rest of us?

We all played together as best we could in our box. Each day we grew bigger, and the space to move was smaller. We also started to get very bored. Sometimes we would fight with each other for something to do. I didn't have any toys, things to chase or chew on, so I liked to chew on my littermates. We squealed and yipped a lot, and I guess we stressed Mom out. She got so mad that she bit me, hard. It hurt my leg and made it bleed. It never did work right after that; it kind of drags, but I can still get around OK. I couldn't believe she would do that to me, but I guess it wasn't her fault. I heard the giant telling another one that sometimes he's seen where the mom will chew off a puppy's tail or even a leg and that this mom wasn't very good anymore, she was six years old and used up, and that she was going to auction where he hoped to get a few bucks for her. I felt bad for Mom. She was so sad. It wasn't her fault; she had tried to be a good dog, but there just wasn't anything to do except lie around in the box and raise puppies. I guess all the fun went out of her life a long time ago.

One day she perked up, her senses on full alert. The box door opened up, and the giant reached in. This time he was after her. She barked at him and tried to bite his hand. We all rushed at the giant's hand too, but he was too big and too fast. He shoved the rest of us away. He got Mom and took her away. I never did see her again, and I'll always wonder what happened to her. Sometimes I still think about her and I miss her.

Then came the day when the big truck stopped and the giant went from box to box and picked out most of the puppies. I tried to flatten myself against the back of the box so that maybe he wouldn't see me, but it didn't work. He got angry and pulled me out by my neck. I saw that I was in a big building that was full of boxes just like mine. There were lots of other puppies, and all of them were barking and whining. It was really scary because I didn't know where my family was, and the giants weren't very nice. I heard one of them say, "This load should get me some good money. Some of 'em are bred already." They grabbed us and threw us into the back of the truck along with lots of other puppies. It was cold and it was dark when they shut the door. I didn't know where I was going, but I knew it couldn't be good. I wished I could be back in my box with my mom and my family.

The noise in the truck was so loud, and it just wouldn't stop. Everyone thought that if they barked loud enough, someone would come and get us out. I knew that wouldn't work because sometimes I used to bark until I was hoarse, and nobody ever came. I couldn't get any sleep. I was cold, and it was hard to breathe.

Some of the puppies and dogs in there with me were sick. They made some terrible messes, and it got all over me, even though I tried to push myself against the sides of the cage to get away. We were packed in very tightly, and there wasn't much room to move.

Each time the truck stopped, the door would open, and the giants would put more puppies into the cages. They didn't seem to care about us much, and we were all scared. We were handled very roughly. I tried to run out one time, but a giant grabbed me and threw me against a cage, and a wire stabbed me in my eye. It hurt so bad I just screamed and cried. I wished Mom was there to help me.

After a long ride, the truck stopped and the door opened. It was so bright I had to squint, but only one eye could close. My other eye felt like it was going to explode. I was so dirty and my coat was all snarled and twisted that it hurt. The giants took a hose and sprayed us all right in our cages. I hadn't had any water for quite a while, so I tried to catch some with my mouth, but I couldn't get much. They put some food in a big pan for us to eat, but some of the other dogs were bigger and stronger, so I didn't get much of that either. Some of them were mean and would bite at me when I tried to get some of the food.

I guess they needed it more than I did.

They hauled us into a big shed with straw bales all around and lots of cages set up on shelves. They put a little rope with a number around my neck. It was very bright in there, and there were lots of giants around. Some of them were smaller giants and lady giants, and some of them talked to me. I don't know what they were saying, but I liked the attention. It was the first time that giants didn't push me around and yell at me or hurt me. They said things like, "Oh, look at this one, her eye is popped, and her leg is broken or something." Some of them looked very sad and tried to touch me, but I backed away because I remembered that giants usually hurt me.

It got really busy with giants all around, sitting on chairs, and then they turned on some kind of machine that made the giants' voices very loud, and the sitting giants got excited. They took some of the puppies out of their cages and held them up for all the giants to see. They told about them and then said some numbers, and then they put the puppies back in their cages. I don't know what that was all about, but I hoped when my turn came, they wouldn't see me. I tried to make myself as small as possible. They got me anyway, and then they took me up in front of all the sitting giants and said, "This cockapoo's a little roughed up, but her momma was a good breeder, and she'll do right by you too. Get a good return on your investment in short order.

She's already bred first time."

There were some lady giants in the front row who said numbers over and over. I watched them and thought that it would be nice to be with them. They kept looking over at some other giants who didn't look nice to me. I liked the lady giants. Soon they stopped saying numbers, and I saw that one of the lady giants was crying. I felt bad for her. Something must have been wrong, and maybe she got hurt.

They put me back in my cage. The noise went on for a long time, and then it stopped. The sitting giants got up, and they started to come get some of us out of our cages. Sometimes the lady giants would get some, and sometimes other giants got them. I recognized one of the lady giants. She stopped at my cage and was crying. She said she was so sorry. She told me she tried to get me but couldn't. I felt so bad for her being so sad. I pushed my face up against the side of the cage and tried to let her know that I would be OK and she shouldn't feel so bad. I wanted to go with her; she seemed very nice and I liked her. I was sad to see her go.

A giant pulled me out of my cage and took me out to a small truck and put me in another cage with some other dogs I never saw before. We were all scared, but it looked like we were going to go for a ride somewhere else. I hoped it would be a nice place, warm and clean and happy. The truck stopped, and the giant carried the cages into a barn. It was kind of dark and very noisy. It reminded me of the place where I used to live with my mom and my brothers *and sisters.* It smelled bad, and there were lots of bigger dogs there too. There were even some boxes just like where I used to live.

One of the giants opened the door to a box and put me in. When the door shut, it was dark. Then the sun came on, and I could see that I had some food and some water, but there was no way to see out. This was not what I wanted. I barked until I was hoarse. I did hear the giant say, "This one'll bring in some money if she lives long enough to give me those pups."

I guess I'm going to live in a box . . . just like Mom.

"Our lives begin to end the day we become silent about things that matter."

—*Martin Luther King Jr.*

CHAPTER 1

MARCH 12, 2008

As Margie and I made our final turn onto a dirt road, on a cold, gray morning, we saw the protestors lined up against the parking-lot entrance, each boasting bright orange clothing, holding signs: one person clinging to a single rusty wire cage stuffed with toy dogs, shouting, "Ban puppy mills."

We pulled into the gravel lot and made our way to the pole barn, walking past Amish buggies, Ford trucks and VW Bugs parked throughout the muddy field. The day was dark, and the auction barn seemed grim. The sign on the door read, "No cameras, no recordings." We entered, completely unaware of what we would see or how we would be seen.

It was never our intent to go in. I had gone as a Web writer for Best Friends Animal Society to report on the protestors. But when I confronted Eilene Ribbens, president and founder of No Wisconsin Puppy Mills, the group leading the protest, she explained, "It's great you're here to report on the protest, but if you really want to know why we're here, you need to walk in that barn and see for yourself. Only then will you fully understand our fight to change things."

I was out of my element. I protested once in high school, twenty years ago, when the administration decided to use the students as pawns for a better contract. My life, that day in March, was nonconfrontational. Sure, I was passionate about animal-welfare issues and worked within my personal realm of comfort to rescue animals, but seeking out protests was definitely not a part of who I was.

As we walked through the barn door, we saw chairs and bleachers set up . . . and to our right were bales of straw, a failed attempt to mask the numerous cages behind them: all filled with dogs.

It was hard not to notice the large influx of both Amish and Mennonites. Dressed in clothing of days gone by, gathered in small groups in the frigid barn: fathers, mothers and obedient children. The pungent smell of fresh-baked bread and dog feces didn't settle my already-queasy stomach.

We slowly made our way past a stage with a speaker system and a podium poised with a gavel atop, and came to an opening in the stacks of straw.

At first glance, my eyes blurred, and everything I saw became a hazy gray. Without any thought and barely a sense of emotion, I looked to my left, and the first dog I saw was a Maltese, a matted ball of white fur. She was huddled in the back of a small plastic carrier with a broken door that was piled on top of other crates full of dogs. She shook on top of wet straw, and her sad eyes pierced mine.

My eyes widened as what lay in front of me came into view: hundreds of dogs in metal cages. No barking. No whining. Some not doing anything—only curled up in the corners of the cages, silently staring away from all of the people.

Cage upon cage, I saw dogs either shaved down to bare skin or with coats so matted it was difficult to identify their breed. Many of the dogs were malnourished, often with infections in their eyes or scars on their bodies. All of them without spirit, without wagging tails. They wouldn't respond to even the friendliest of hands. They were broken, and it broke my heart.

Dachshunds, Maltese, Chihuahuas, West Highland white terriers, Yorkshire terriers, French bulldogs, bichons, poodles, beagles, Shih Tzus, miniature pinschers, and many more.

Each dog had a rope tied around its neck, with a cattle number attached that coincided to the listings in the auction catalog—which boasted a pretty little Maltese with a bow in her hair. There weren't any dogs who looked like that.

#171 was the oldest dog at the auction. He was listed as a Chinese crested and a "proven" breeder. All I saw was desperation in his eyes.

We went from cage to cage, trying to engage the dogs—quietly hoping that our sincere voices and gentle touch would raise their spirits: there were so many. Had the circumstances been different, I would have been in heaven, surrounded by hundreds of dogs, but instead, it felt like hell on earth.

The cages, many piled on each other, some standing above the ground on metal posts, were all made of chicken wire—even the bottoms. None of the dogs had anything soft, smooth or even solid to walk or lie down on. Each cube was the size of a rabbit cage. No food, no water, and certainly, no toys.

Occasionally I took my eyes off the dogs and peered around the area. I watched the Amish and Mennonites handle their stock and observed people who looked like me ask questions, referring back to the auction booklet. Everything around me felt silent, even with hundreds of people scurrying about the rows of dogs.

Without any direction, not one clue of what to do, we kept to ourselves. I felt out of place: we didn't belong. I questioned it all. Were people like us supposed to be here? Could we get thrown out? Though we were crammed in lines to see the dogs, I had never felt so alone.

Only hours earlier, Margie and I were imagining what the day would bring. It was a four-hour drive, and even though we were walking in blind, we had so much to talk about. One of our biggest questions was if we would rescue any dogs.

"Do you think you'll take any home?" Margie asked.

"Gosh no! Bill would kill me. We already have so many since I worked at the county shelter. I think we're done taking in homeless animals," I said, knowing it sounded colder than I meant.

"Well, I brought the kennel, just in case."

I could feel her compassion and was reassured by her willingness to walk into a completely unknown situation and be prepared for whatever might come our way.

"The truth is, I don't even know if we can go in, or if people like us can get any of the dogs. Margie, I don't know one single thing about this. How crazy is that?" I wondered out loud.

"Gosh, what if we can take dogs? There might be hundreds. How would you know which one to pick? Do you think you could pick just one?"

I became dizzy at the thought.

"Well, you know me," Margie said. "I love dachshunds. I wonder if there will be any of them?"

Margie was involved in doxie rescue. She had a few of her own and often helped with transports and home visits. I envied that if it came down to getting any dogs, her focus would be on one breed. For me, just about any dog was a possibility.

"How *will* we pick just one? How bad do you think it'll be, if we can go in?" she asked.

Neither of us had any idea.

After hours of conversation, we came to the conclusion that we wouldn't get any. We just wouldn't.

But we also agreed to only go into the barn for a quick look, and found ourselves mesmerized by it all: the crammed cages, the people looking for "stock," and the horrible truth standing in front of us: puppy mills did exist. The next thing I knew, Margie had made a list of the doxies she found herself drawn to, and she was getting her license from the car so we would have a bidding number.

Margie and I had been friends for a few years. When I started thinking about who to beg to attend the auction protest with me, I immediately thought of her. She loved dogs and believed in the importance of rescuing them. She was also a fighter for the truth. I knew she would offer strength to me in a time of uncertainty. The auction proved to be that kind of time.

I stayed in the barn, completely alone alongside dozens of people, and continued walking in circles from cage to cage, thinking back to just two years ago when I walked into my county shelter to volunteer. I had been so eager to help and yet so afraid of what truths I would find: the number of dogs who were homeless, or worse, the number of dogs who were euthanized every day.

In search of a way to make a difference and follow my true passion, I held my breath and filled out the volunteer application. In two weeks, I was volunteering almost daily, and in six months, I was working there part-time. I had seen both horrors and miracles, but nothing that ever came close to what was staring me in the face.

I looked into the cages of two beagles who wouldn't turn their heads to meet my gaze. I leaned down to the bent-up crate, lying in the dirty straw strewn across the cold cement floor. Not knowing if it was allowed, I placed my hand carefully in between the metal bars and touched #191, who shared the cramped space with another beagle, #192, his fur dirty and coarse. No reaction. He didn't even look at me; he didn't even flinch. I began to pet him; no wagging tail. I spoke to him. Still no reaction. I tried everything I knew to engage him, but he stayed crouched in the corner of the cage.

No, it was nothing like walking dogs or even cleaning kennels at the county shelter—nothing at all. Never before had I seen two dogs stare right past me as though I weren't even there. Dogs at the county shelter jumped on the kennel doors to grab attention. They screamed "adopt me" with their wagging tails and loud barks. They were eager for human attention. These dogs were not.

A Mennonite man tapped my shoulder and said it was time for me to take my seat. When I looked around, I realized that I was the only one left among the cages.

I walked by the rows of cold, rusty cages one last time as I made my way out of the stacks—imagining myself at a pet store, looking innocently into the eyes of a playful pup behind the glass, now knowing that this WAS where they all came from.

I desperately looked up for Margie, who had found us a seat on one of the back bleachers. She raised her hand slightly to wave towards me, and I smiled, realizing that I wasn't alone anymore. I walked towards her, glancing at the rest of the faces staring back at me and wondering why they were here.

In minutes, the loudspeaker blared and the auction started. No one was allowed back to see the animals anymore. The gavel came down, and the first item hit the auction table: a dog bed.

A warm and fuzzy dog bed. The irony hit me, and I could barely breathe.

For thirty minutes, products hit the auction table: leashes, bowls, beds, even toys. I was most surprised to see a microchip scanner auctioned off.

For a few moments, my heart was beating again and my stomachache had nearly faded until I saw the little Maltese, the first dog I had seen, brought up and dumped on the table.

A dirty white fur ball of a dog, who shook uncontrollably. Never looking up towards the people, she kept her face hidden under her paws. The auctioneer said, "Number 1, female Maltese born 2/10/06. Checks good—is a good mother—ready to make you money."

On the auction sheet, each dog had a registration number. Some were with the American Kennel Club (AKC) and others were with America's Pet Registry (APRI). These weren't just mutts or accidental puppies. These dogs were registered with organizations, meaning that they would come with papers. The kind of papers dog owners like to brag about when they get a purebred.

I had never seen such an innocent creature and felt such a raw vulnerability. It was unbearably unsettling. I felt like someone had punched me hard in the stomach. Tears welled up in my eyes. My jaw was clenched. Everything around me became quiet and distant, as though I were floating about the crowd, looking from high above. It was only me and the Maltese, and an incredible sense of helplessness.

The bidding began. Starting at twenty-five dollars and quickly rising to over $500, with a Mennonite man winning the dog. Once the dog was won, they would take it back to the cages. No dog left until the money was collected.

"Number 2, male Maltese born 3/5/05— checks good—proven breeder."

One by one, each dog was auctioned off just like the beds and the collars were. Later, I would come to the realization that the auction didn't start with products: they were all products.

The slogan Best Friends had coined for the campaign against the puppy mills was, "Puppies are not products." And, of course, that was what my protest sign read, the sign which was sitting in the back of my car.

Margie and I sat in the bleachers, trying to figure everyone out. Were there rescuers here? Who were they? The Amish and the Mennonites' dress made it easy to identify them, but the others, in regular street clothes, left us wondering; who was here to save and who was here to continue the cycle of cruelty?

There were children and families and people eating concessions. It was actually a family event for many in the audience. I just couldn't fathom enjoying one moment of it. My stomach was upside down with complete disgust—food was the last thing on my mind.

Dachshunds were up next, and Margie showed me on the back of the bidding card the numbers of the doxies she wanted to save. There were six.

Only hours ago, we weren't bringing home any dogs, and now Margie had her list of six. I didn't question her change of heart one bit, even though we never said a word about it to each other. We hadn't talked much at all since entering the barn. Much of our time was spent separate from one another, staring into dogs' cages. The reality that lay in front of us was so horribly powerful, no words could adequately portray it. We didn't discuss anything, just reacted. And as two dog lovers, who, in theory, weren't taking any dogs home, there were no words needed between us to understand that both of us would do anything to save just one.

The auctioneer shouted, "Number 5, male dachshund, checks good. Start at one hundred dollars."

Without hesitation, Margie raised her bidding number. The auctioneer took the bid, and from there it went on for two minutes. All the doxies went above Margie's invisible price limit. We had no idea what we were doing. We didn't even know what prices we were willing to pay. And yet, we were trying to learn the game and figure out all of the players.

One breed at a time, the dogs were auctioned. They would go from twenty dollars to over $1000, with the French bulldogs taking in the most money. All of them seemed to go to the same Mennonite man. We hadn't figured out which side he was on. We were too naive to see the truth in front of us.

Some of the females auctioned off were in heat or even pregnant. The Mennonite auctioneer would announce, "This one is ready to make you money." Most of the dogs were a year old or younger.

Not #171. He was the oldest dog at the auction—and it showed. He was the one I was waiting for.

When I had opened his cage to pet him, he eventually came to the front and ever so gently licked my fingers. When I slowly went to pet him, I felt nothing but mats. His entire coat was knotted—a stinky mess. I had worked in the county shelter for a year and a half, and never had I seen anything like him.

He was listed as a Chinese crested powder puff, a breed I didn't even know existed; and I had always prided myself on my knowledge of dog breeds. He was a dirty white with gray on his ears and large gray spots on his back. In the few places that weren't matted, his fur was long and stringy. His ears seemed awfully big for his small head. I guessed he weighed around twelve pounds, but it was hard to tell his true body size since I couldn't begin to feel his ribs or stomach beneath the knotted fur. And he smelled, bad.

However, the truth was that how he looked didn't matter. Not his color, or his breed, his sex or his age. It was his gentle soul I noticed more than anything. The way he licked my hand, the way his eyes looked up at me. Never, after years of animal interaction, had I felt so connected to a dog.

I could hear our conversation, "If you did get one, how would you know which one to pick?" It seemed a senseless thing to say after finding #171. In my mind and in my heart, I knew he needed to get out. And, so, I waited. . . .

Every now and then, a family would win the bid and jump for joy over their new puppy. It seemed to me an odd place to get a family dog, but truthfully, it would have been the same dog in a pet store for possibly twice the price.

For the most part, they went in numeric order, and #171 was near the end. Maybe that was a good thing. I was focused on him, so I wasn't as tempted to randomly bid on others. And I believe my desire to save him was what got me through the three horrible hours.

CHAPTER 2

ALWAYS AN ANIMAL ADVOCATE

Overcome with panic and dismay, my thoughts began to drift: What had led me down this path and to an event that I could only think of as a horror movie?

Just a few months ago, I was content living in suburbia: volunteering at my daughter's school and driving her to soccer, my husband coming home each night for dinner and all of us going to Dairy Queen for dessert.

None of that changed, but I changed, and found myself becoming enthralled with animal welfare. First, I gave my time to a wildlife sanctuary; then, I had an actual paid position as a kennel tech at my local animal control; and next, I was volunteering as a network writer for Best Friends Animal Society, a national organization founded in Utah. THE organization responsible for taking twenty-two of Michael Vick's pit bulls.

A recent news tip offered me an opportunity to report on a dog auction in Thorp, Wisconsin. I took the story with little reservation.

I have always loved animals—all animals. I think I rescued my first stray dog at age eight. I found a scruffy yellow mutt wandering the neighborhood and then went house to house until I found its home.

Walking turtles across the street and creating frog habitats was second nature to me. One of my most memorable animal stories was when my best friend, Kelly, and I raised two orphan ducklings one summer. We would take them for buggy rides in our doll strollers. People would stop to see our dolls and be shocked to find two ducks nestled in pink blankets with bonnets on their heads. We liked to think that we taught them how to swim. Eventually, we took them to a haven where ducks could swim in ponds and wander freely among themselves.

A more bizarre story was when Kelly, Mary Kate and I housed tent caterpillars. We had coffee cans labeled, "Retirement home," "Nursery," "Teens" and "Parents," each caterpillar segregated by what age we assumed it to be. When the caterpillars would die, we would hold a caterpillar funeral. We'd wrap them in tissue, place them in a baggie and hold a ceremony with cookies (for us) in their honor.

Then there were the guinea-pig picnics we would go on, taking our guinea pigs by bike to the neighborhood park. Packing crackers and carrots and letting them frolic in the grass as we, their mothers, talked and ate our lunch. For some reason, we really believed that they enjoyed going down the slide.

I think the last guinea-pig picnic was around junior high. Then, instead of animals, there were cheerleading, proms and boys. All along, I cherished our family dogs, but saving animals took a backseat to growing up.

Soon, I was in college, studying human resources and family development at the University of Illinois. I graduated and began work as a human resources assistant at a manufacturing plant. In pursuit of a successful career, I went on to earn a master's degree in human resource management and soon became the manager of the entire department. I loved so much of my job, but there was always a tugging at my heart, pulling me to the very thing I'd always been passionate about.

At the age of thirty, I went through a divorce, and maybe that critical event pushed me to really question what I wanted in life. When I remarried about five years later, it became clear there was nothing more important than following my heart and being true to myself.

So, I left my job and ventured into animal welfare.

However, the auction wasn't exactly what I had in mind. I had just gotten over all of the heartbreak of euthanasia I experienced at animal control. I hated saying good-bye to my position at the shelter, but I couldn't take any more of the emotionally crippling pain. I chose to get away from the hands-on because it hurt too much.

Yet, there I was in a cold barn, witnessing things I had only seen on Animal Planet. But I was there, and I already knew the reason was much bigger than me.

CHAPTER 3

#171

After nearly three hours of never moving from my hard seat on the bleachers, I caught the young Amish boy taking #171 out of his cage. As he grabbed him by the rope around his neck and pulled #171 toward him, the dog stretched out his legs, yanking back like a mule. The boy gave him one last tug, and #171 hung stiff in the air until the boy flung him under his arm and carried him to the auction table—where the supposed vet, another Mennonite, looked him over from a stone's throw away.

I burst out, "There he is, Margie, that's him." I had already grown attached. There were nearly three hundred dogs at the auction, and then, there was #171. I had spent over an hour going cage to cage, touching, feeling, talking to dogs I didn't know and would probably never see again. I opened crate doors and looked into hundreds of pairs of eyes. None of them spoke to me like #171.

He was the first one for whom I had enough courage to actually open the cage door when no one was looking. I didn't know if that was acceptable, or if I was breaking any of the unwritten rules that seemed to fill the barn with heavy, stagnant air. All I knew was that I needed to touch him, to make contact with him, to somehow make things different for him, for me, for everything about the day.

I had looked around, scouting out any of "them," and without further hesitation gently opened the cage door. #171 stood frozen, staring at me, rigid and unflinching. I put my hand by his nose to smell and got no reaction. I slowly moved my hand to his head and touched him, feeling nothing but cemented fur, smelling nothing but manure, seeing nothing that resembled any dog I ever knew.

My hand came back to his face and hung for a while in the air, between the two of us, waiting for some sign, and then, at the moment I was about to take it away, this small pink tongue emerged. Like a lost pup who found his mom, he licked me. There was no turning back.

Eilene Ribbens, the protest leader outside, had told us when we asked how she felt about people rescuing the dogs, "If you take a dog out of there today, the best thing you can do is make sure to make a story out of him. Show the people how he looks, what his illnesses are, how he behaves. Don't let his story go untold."

And so it was. During the auction, I named him Thorp. It was the town the auction was held in, and it seemed to fit him. Later, I would wonder if giving him that name would hinder his future; naming him after his past. I would decide that truly, it is not our past that defines us but what we make of our future. That would be Thorp—a dog with a new future.

There were two dogs ahead of Thorp, and I had been thinking: What if I was about to bid against a rescuer? I wouldn't want them to pay more than they had to. Margie and I had no real proof that there were any rescuers present, but there had been a lot of evidence to suggest that there were rescuers there. There was one woman who always seemed to bid on the ones in bad shape. We were fairly certain she was with a rescue, or at least we wanted her to be.

It was accurate for us to reason that the Amish and the Mennonites were there to buy for their businesses and the English were there to rescue.

Without hesitation and with newfound courage, I got out of my seat and practically ran to the woman's chair, where she was seated close to the podium. I sat next to her and in seconds blurted out, "Are you a rescuer?"

Hesitant to reveal her purpose to me, she asked, "Who are you?"

My heart was beating a mile a minute. In my fastest speech, I explained my purpose as a writer for Best Friends. I told her that I was interested in saving the Chinese crested, and I just didn't want to bid against her.

Satisfied with my answer, she told me, "Yes, I am a rescuer."

A feeling of pure relief came over me. It was the first time that day I actually felt a sense of comfort. She explained that she was low on funds to save him, but thought that the Chinese Crested Rescue would take him.

As she spoke, I could hear the auctioneer repeat the words I had heard all day. This time they had the most meaning. "Number 171, Chinese crested, checks good." So, I bid. #171 started at twenty dollars, and with heartfelt determination and not a lot of interest from anyone there, I "won" #171 for sixty dollars.

It still breaks my heart.

I didn't recognize myself, running across a crowded room of strangers, blurting things out. I was never shy, but in unfamiliar situations I was always comfortable staying in the background. My desire to change #171's life opened up a part of me. It gave me the strength to disregard my hesitations, and because of that, we had broken through the invisible wall. As I sat next to the auction table and saw the dogs up close, I was part of it all. I was no longer an onlooker. All of a sudden, the auction became a part of who I was.

In minutes, Margie joined me next to my new "friend," Carol. Rescuers were appearing from all sides of the barn to meet us. We were suddenly part of the circle. It felt good to no longer be the outsiders.

Instantly, they were telling us who rescued what—there were rescuers representing nearly all of the breeds. Thankfully, all the doxies Margie was concerned with went to rescue. We were exchanging e-mails and backgrounds and learning so much about the entire ring.

But while we were sitting there, actually making friends amid the travesty of the day, more dogs were being auctioned. It was nearing the end. The mixed breeds known to consumers as "designer dogs" were on the table. Margie kept pushing me to bid, and in an unexplainable action, I "won" another dog: a bichon-poo.

I openly admit that it was an irresponsible thing to do. #171 was more than I could handle. I had no idea what I would do with another one. But I had become caught up in the moment. The greed, the horror, the pain and then the miracle of rescuers. My head was spinning, and my common sense was lost.

The auction ended, and we began friendships with a group of concerned and caring rescuers. They had started the circle at a previous auction in the same barn. Just as I had feared bidding against a rescuer, they had all previously communicated at the last auction and agreed to wear turtlenecks as a subtle way to identify themselves. Everyone was making plans for even better communication before the next auction in the fall.

I got in line to pay for the two lives I was so proud to save and yet so anxious about. I had no idea what I had gotten myself into.

I stood with Carol as other rescuers came forward and quietly explained who they were. I felt a sense of relief but also noticed that being a rescuer was still something covert.

Carol explained as we waited, "Shh . . . they don't want rescuers here. They don't want us involved in their business or any of this. If you take anything too far, like take photos or make a complaint, they'll kick you out."

I gasped for air as I felt like I was doing something illegal.

Most of the people in the line to pay were Amish or Mennonite. I watched as they paid for their new stock and went to the stacks of cages to retrieve it.

They didn't cuddle the dogs. They just grabbed them and stuck them in another crate. There were no blankets on the cold day; there were no food or treats. They would fill a crate with the different breeds they had purchased and load up the buggy or the truck and vanish.

As I stood in line, still attempting to take it all in, I noticed on one side of the barn a large contraption similar to a supersized hamster wheel.

Carol caught my stare and asked, "Want to know what that is?"

"Yes," I whispered.

"It's an exercise wheel they attach to a mill cage. Since the dogs never go outside to play or walk on grass to pee, the wheel gives them something to do."

As my jaw dropped, she added, "And only a few mill dogs even get that."

The woman in front of me was a humane officer from Vilas County, Wisconsin. We talked, and she said how she wished she could save more, but only had a limited budget.

Without hesitating, I blurted, "Would you want the bichon-poo I bought? I really have no idea what I'm doing here."

She said, "I would love to! At the last auction, we rescued a large group of dogs. The auction had been on a Saturday, and by Monday afternoon, we had adopted out all the dogs or had them in foster homes. People are already waiting for us to get back to help these dogs."

The Thorp auction was held twice a year in March and September. (I learned later that the auction day was changed from Saturday to Wednesday to make it more difficult for rescuers and protestors to attend. Most of the people in those groups had full-time jobs during the regular workweek.)

I was relieved. It had been a roller coaster of emotions all day, but in the last hour of the auction, we became part of a small group of people doing their best to make a difference—to change the fate of the dogs. I became part of something bigger. For a brief moment, I felt like I could breathe again.

I proudly paid for my rescues and eagerly went to find them. I found the bichon-poo, opened his cage door and patted him on the head. Softly, I said to him, "I got you out, no more for you. I bet a family is already waiting to love you. Good luck."

I brought the bichon to the Vilas County rescuer. She told me, "He'll go fast. We have so many seniors who want dogs just like him."

I snuggled him one last time and wished him a good, well-deserved new life. It was a perfect ending to a horrible beginning for the fuzzy little guy.

Then, without pause, I made my way to #171. My heart was racing, and tears were welling up in my eyes. I went to him in his cage and said, "It's over. The hell is over for you. I promise that everything is going to be OK."

Tears were streaming down my cold cheeks. I asked the Mennonite man if I could have MY pup. I showed him my paper, and he unchained the cage door, yanked the dog free and dropped him in my arms.

#171 was shaking and licking my finger. He was in such bad shape. His entire body was matted about an inch or more thick. I could see bits of straw and feces woven into the knots of fur. As I held him close, I could smell something rancid, but after one look in his eyes, nothing else mattered.

Though I was holding him and feeling grateful that I could change his fate, it was still painful to look around and see many more whose fate probably hadn't changed. I knew who the millers were now and saw them grab their dogs. I knew that many of the dogs leaving here would go to yet another cage in another cold barn and wait until the next auction or…worse.

Many rescuers came up to us and thanked us for getting #171 out. "He needed to be saved, he was the oldest one." "Look at how bad his fur is." "Thank God he gets a chance for a new life."

I held #171 tighter and looked away from the others. My nerves were shot and I could not take much more.

Margie and I said our good-byes to all the wonderful people we had met and made our plans to come back in the fall. Carol had befriended a Mennonite man who owned a puppy mill. He asked if she would come to his farm and take more Chihuahua puppies. She agreed to go, along with four other rescuers.

Once out of the auction barn, back into the crisp air and the muddy lot, Margie stopped me and took my and Thorp's first picture together: the auction barn in the background, the "no cameras" sign posted on the door.

Thorp was silent, no whining, no barking, nothing at all. Squeezed between my arms, his body felt stiff and unwavering. He would look up at me, but only for moments, and then his eyes would drift away—away from me, away from it all.

It was possibly the first picture Thorp ever had taken. My stomach was in knots. I was filled first with despair and then hope as I looked down at the matted, dirty, depressed dog I was so unprepared to take home.

Against my better judgment earlier in the day, Margie had convinced me that we should bring a large dog carrier, "just in case." As she was opening it now for Thorp, I was busy looking for a sweatshirt to place in it. I had become so hardened in the last few hours that I assumed the carrier didn't have anything soft.

Margie stopped me. "I placed a blanket and some toys in the carrier before we left," she said softly, as though she understood why I was surprised.

Of course she did. It is what animal lovers do. I was in such a fog. My reality and the hell I had witnessed had meshed, and I was left unsure of anything.

I put Thorp in the carrier. He was shaking but he didn't fight. He didn't do anything. I put the carrier in the backseat. He sat up in it and didn't move or make a peep.

Once we were all settled in the car, we drove away. Most of the cars and all of the buggies were gone. Only a protest sign lay in the dirt reading, "No more mills."

Seeing it, I caught my breath.

The day had come and gone. In just hours, what I knew about life had changed forever. It was crueler than I was ready to face. But now, in the back of my car, sat a dog who would remind me of everything I had seen, an entire world I wanted to forget. As I looked in the rearview mirror and caught his eyes, I knew that something bigger was ahead of me.

CHAPTER 4

HOME

One glance at the time and suddenly I remembered my other life. I knew I needed to call my husband, Bill. In the three short years we had been married, he had grown to accept my passion for animals. At the time, we had two rescue dogs and four rescue cats.

In October of 2007, we lost our dog, Digger, in a car accident. We were at our summer home, and while everyone was disembarking the boat, Digger ran into the busy street. We were traumatized.

We had driven three hours to a county shelter in Indiana for Digger. I had found him on Petfinder.com. He was in horrendous shape. When we met Digger at the shelter, he wobbled out of a dirty old crate, matted and stinky, walked over to a small scrap of carpet and peed. Bill looked at me and said, "This is who we came for?"

He had been completely neglected. His coat was grossly matted, but worse, he had no understanding of love or affection. We only had Digger three years before we lost him. He had come so far—seeking attention and enjoying snuggling with us.

He never seemed able to understand potty training, but we loved him anyway. Somehow, through it all, Digger had become Bill's dog, and he was still recovering from the loss.

We had talked about getting another dog, but I never really considered the auction.

The phone rang and rang, and finally Bill answered it with his usual work voice, "Hello, this is Bill."

"Hi, honey. We made it through the auction," I said, knowing that unless he was there, he would never come to realize what making it through a dog auction meant.

I had no idea how to start the conversation or how to even describe what we had seen. It was as though we had survived some kind of disaster. I knew right then I would never be able to effectively convey to others what I had witnessed. But I knew I had to try.

After some small talk about it all, Bill said, "Well, it's quiet. That's a good sign; no dogs barking."

I swallowed hard and said, "Well, he *is* just quiet."

There was silence on the phone.

"What?" Bill muttered.

"I did it. I got one. We had to get this one out. He was the oldest and in the worse shape." Without stopping, I kept rambling on, "And anyway, there is a rescue that will take him. I just have to keep him until they have room."

It wasn't a lie. The Chinese Crested Rescue did want him. But my heart already loved him and I knew he had to be mine.

Bill's silence spoke volumes, but I believed with all of my soul, I was doing the right thing. I felt bad that my husband was disappointed, but this wasn't just about a dog to me. This was about finding my purpose and believing I could make a difference to Thorp and to this cause. Not doing anything didn't seem like an option.

I might never know or be able to explain how I knew to save Thorp. Something, someone had spoken to me. I took a leap and jumped in. There was no turning back.

The car ride was short and long, tiring and thrilling. Margie and I didn't know what to say, yet silence was unbearable. There was so much to make sense of and so little we could grasp. It was exhausting, and yet I was so energized.

The day had ripped open my soul, but I had never felt so whole or so sure of myself and my purpose.

The tears I hadn't cried all day seemed to be building my courage. They were smoldering inside of me, building into a fire I would soon be fighting.

Throughout the ride, I would look back at Thorp. He never lay down. I envisioned him assuming he was on his way to another cage, another cold and cruel barn. I wondered how many auctions he had been bought and sold at. How many times his life remained sadly unchanged.

This time was finally different for him, and he didn't even know it.

We stopped once for gas and snacks. I tried to feed him a morsel of cheese, but he just licked it and let it drop from his mouth. I tried to give him a taste of water, but he just looked away.

He was so disengaged. It broke my heart, and it kind of scared me. What on earth was I doing?

I was more anxious the closer we got to home. Was Bill really mad? What would I do with this dog? Did he have any contagious diseases? Would my dogs like him?

I was mentally sketching a plan. My second call was to my groomer. In a shaky voice, I explained to Mark that I had just rescued a mill dog, and I needed to know if there was any way they could take him first thing in the morning, as he was in bad shape. Of course they could, Mark said. After a day full of inhumanity, the kind gestures of people who loved animals seemed to ease my broken heart.

Amid the grief and the day's painful events, I still had to figure out what to do when I got home with a dog I didn't know. Until that day, I never even knew a Chinese crested powder puff existed. I decided I would put Thorp in the laundry room, which could serve as a pseudo quarantine. My time at the shelter taught me the importance of quarantine. Not knowing anything about Thorp or the illnesses found in puppy mills, it would be critical to keep him away from the rest of the family until he saw my vet. I would leave the other two dogs in the bedroom and prepare the room: food, water, and a bed. My head was just spinning. And there was so much more to think about.

After five hours, we arrived at Margie's house and showed her fiancé, Chris, our rescue. It was dark and late, so it was hard for him to see. Chris mentioned that he had taken Bill out for a few beers to ease the pain of the new dog. I gulped, dreading going home.

The drive from Margie's seemed longer than usual. My heart was racing, and my thoughts scattered. In the back of my car was a dog I knew nothing about. A dog who came with issues I had no experience with. A dog who was not crying, or panting, or doing anything at all—only sitting stiffly in the back of my car, MY car.

Thorp and I pulled into the driveway, the very place I had pulled out of less than thirty-six hours ago. The outside lights were on, but everything else was dark and quiet. Our two dogs barked, acknowledging my entrance.

I brought Thorp inside the house in his carrier. His body shook uncontrollably. I closed the laundry-room door and set down the carrier. With caution, I opened the kennel door, and he slowly crept out.

His eyes blinked as they adjusted to the light. His body cowered and his tail curled under. One small step at a time. If I made any noise or small movement, he would retreat back inside the crate.

I waited. I took small breaths and stayed as still as possible. There was an unspoken relationship between the dog and myself. We didn't need words. We both just needed time.

Each time that Thorp crept out of the cage and stepped into the laundry room, I felt more confident that this could make sense, that I could do this, whatever "this" was.

Not patient by nature, this was very different for me. I was already committed.

As Thorp took in the laundry-room surroundings, I got him a bowl of water. He flinched as I set it down and remained resistant and unsure. Cautiously, he looked into the water bowl and then drank like there was no tomorrow. He was so thirsty. I wondered when he had drunk last. There wasn't any water in the cages at the auction.

I went back to the car to gather some things, and when I came in, Thorp was on his back legs, dancing! He was looking up at me and prancing. To me, it was a celebration dance for his freedom.

I gently put a noose leash around his neck and took him outside. He didn't understand the leash and thrashed about like a wild horse being broken, but he seemed to enjoy the grass. Thorp took one step at a time, lifting and shaking each foot after it touched the ground. The stairs were foreign to him, but slowly, he showed signs of confidence by climbing each step. When his paws would touch the snow, he would frighten and jump away. He peed in a few places to mark his territory.

I found myself talking to him—more than to any other dog I had rescued in the past. It was as though I needed to explain everything to him. In reality, I think I was explaining everything to myself. An attempt to understand what had just happened to my life and unconsciously realizing my life would never again be the same.

Once we were back inside, I sat down on the floor, and Thorp plopped right in my lap and kissed my face. He was still shaking and nervous, but somehow knew to trust me. I talked to him and told him that the hell was over as I took off the livestock rope tied around his neck, with the cattle tag stamped "171."

As if it were the Hilton, I made him a bed for kings. Fluffed mattress, clean blankets and a teddy bear to keep him company, all of which were probably the first such items he ever had. I showed him his food and left him for the night.

He never made a sound.

CHAPTER 5

DAY ONE

Thorp remained silent, but my night was not so relaxing. I tossed and turned and dreamed and woke up. I was exhausted from the drive, emotionally spent from the experience. Life as I knew it would never be the same again, and that was anything but settling.

The entire day played in my head each time I tried to close my eyes. The Amish and the Mennonites, once known to me as kinder, gentler people, now seemed so cruel as they represented all of the puppy millers at the auction.

The crates of dogs lined up, one right after the other. The straw, the stench, the fresh-baked bread. The auctioneer and the gavel. The protestors in orange, the rescuers. It was impossible to sleep, knowing there were dogs who didn't get rescued—and even worse, thousands of dogs living like that as I slept in my posh king-size bed.

Tears rolled down my face, just one at a time until I drifted off to sleep—the only place I could find peace, and that was only if I didn't have to face the nightmares.

It seemed that I passed out from pure exhaustion, but the night found me tossing and turning. Visions of dogs and hay and Amish people still rattled in my head as my eyes opened to the morning light. And I couldn't hide from the fact that downstairs, just seventeen steps away, was this alien dog.

A dog I had no idea how to care for.

I rolled over and petted the two dogs I did know: Buddy and Sadie. While both had been rescued, neither, to my knowledge, ever experienced what the dogs I saw at the auction did. I had never experienced anything like that.

My chest felt tight, and it was all I could do not to throw up. I found my courage and my strength to get out of bed and face the choices I had made the day before.

It was time to check on the dog who I now called Thorp.

As I walked down the steps to the laundry room, there were no sounds. Complete silence. I will never forget walking down those stairs—each one closer not just to a dog I had randomly decided to take home, but also to the reality of everything I had seen the day before.

With a deep breath, I opened the door.

In a corner, he was huddled. Lying on the towel I had given him. He didn't make eye contact, but I saw his tail wiggle as I quietly said, "Good morning, Thorp."

I gently walked to him. I was careful not to make sudden movements. I knelt down by his side and let him smell me. He inched his way to my lap and sat down in it and shook. I stroked his back and spoke words that at least comforted me.

Any sudden movement and he instantly trembled. A noise, even a whisper sent him back to the corner, his safe zone. He really had no understanding of this kind of life. And I had no understanding of a dog so messed up. Tears rolled down my cheeks. I was completely lost. I'd never experienced such cruelty. Never seen a dog so broken and never felt so alone. No one I knew would be able to comprehend what I had witnessed. I didn't think any of my friends would be able to feel my loss. I was scared just like Thorp. Neither of us knew what lay ahead in the next minute or hour or days to come. Both of our lives felt uncomfortably changed.

I took him outside. The stairs weren't as scary, and he hopped up them a little quicker than the night before.

I noticed that he ate some of the food I had left him and drank more water.

We got ready to go to the groomer. He backed away as I put on his leash and opened the door to the garage. Thorp just sat and shook. He didn't want to leave. I picked him up, trying to reassure him. He remained rigid. I set him on the blanket in the front seat, and he continued to shake. He quivered the whole car ride.

I parked the car and opened the door as Thorp sat staring out the window. I gently picked him up, and he stayed frozen and shaking in my arms, not making a sound. He smelled awful. His coat was compacted with straw, dirt and feces.

I opened the door to the groomer's, and Mark, the owner, smiled, but his eyes widened when he saw Thorp. Leslie-Anne, his wife, came from the back, laughing. "Who did you rescue this time?"

But her voice trailed off as she got a glimpse of Thorp. "Oh my God," she exhaled. "We can't save his coat. It has to be shaved. This is horrendous."

I had no words. I couldn't muster a sound. I didn't know what to say—where to begin. It was all like a bad dream. Forty-eight hours earlier, I was simply dropping my daughter off at school. Now, I was at the groomer with a puppy-mill dog . . . What I'd seen, the people I'd met, the underground world I had discovered and become a part of. There were no words. None.

Luckily, I didn't need any. Mark and Leslie-Anne knew. As I handed over my rescued pup, I felt like I was betraying the small bit of trust I'd earned from him. Thorp looked back at me, and it melted my broken heart. In my mind's eye, I snapped a picture— as if the moment wasn't already burned into my soul.

The short drive home was a blur. I felt like I held my breath the whole time. It was as if breathing made it all real. I wasn't ready for it to be real. I needed time. Time to comprehend, to wrap my head around the last twenty-four hours.

***

While Thorp was being groomed, I had a story to report. It was my assignment to detail the auction, though the original story was just supposed to be about the protestors. It had all become so much more than that. I didn't even know where to start, so I just began describing it, reliving each horrible moment. Taking people through the cages, hearing the auctioneer, not hearing the dogs.

I was riveted as I typed. In shock that I had been there at all. A place I had never imagined. A place that only days earlier had seemed unbelievable. I wrote from my heart as I played out a day in my life I could never begin to forget.

By afternoon, the story was live on the Internet, and the readers' comments were pouring in. People saying that they were in tears. That they had no idea. They couldn't fathom it. And people were thanking me for going, for sharing and for speaking the truth, as raw and as real as it all was.

A few hours later, I was back to pick up Thorp. When Leslie-Anne brought him out and I saw his tiny, trembling body, totally shaved down to bare skin, I started to cry. His frail frame looked so naked and so cold. He had to be terrified. He'd probably never been groomed his whole life.

Mark handed me a plastic bag of Thorp's fur. His entire coat had been shaved off in one solid piece. Not one ounce of it could have been saved. A life's worth of pain and neglect, all in a plastic bag. They gave him a bright blue collar that someone once donated—and I started to cry. Generosity seemed so obscure after the auction.

Thorp snuggled up to my chest. He looked even more broken, but brand-new. He had his own collar and a bright blue bandana, and for a brief moment, I saw him as a normal dog. In the car, I took his picture, and I swear he was smiling.

The day continued—it almost seemed never-ending. E-mails flooded in from the rescuers I had met. Everyone was recapping the day's events. Many detailed the dogs they got and the conditions they were in—none of them good. A few of the dogs were pregnant.

Margie and I talked on the phone. It was as though it were only she and I in the world. She was the only person who knew how much I hurt inside and how shaken to the core I felt. Everyone else close to me seemed irrelevant because they didn't understand and couldn't relate.

Bill had called during the day. "What's the plan for tonight? Any thoughts on dinner?" he asked nonchalantly.

Finding my voice despite the tears rolling down my cheeks, I answered, "Uh, I hadn't thought about dinner."

"I was thinking cheesy chicken sounded good. Oh, could you pick me up some shaving cream? Kinda running low."

Before I could reply, he said, "Hey, gotta run, I have a meeting in ten about the new offices. Love you."

"Love you, too." My voice trailed off.

Cheesy chicken, shaving cream, new offices. His words sailed around my head, so light and free. It was just another day for him. While I wasn't angry with him, it was painfully frustrating to feel unheard.

He didn't know my world had shifted. He didn't know I was treading water to get through the day. He didn't know people across the country were being brought to tears by my news story of the auction. He didn't know, but I needed him to.

It was around five p.m., and I knew Bill would be home. I hadn't faced him last night, and he didn't have much to say on the phone when we talked.

Thorp stayed in the laundry room all day. It was important that he stay away from the other dogs, at least until I knew if he had any of the contagious diseases the rescuers had warned me of, because of the conditions mill dogs live in and their lack of veterinary care. Buddy and Sadie lay outside the door, sniffing and wagging their tails, anxious to meet the furry stranger in the house.

The garage door went up, and my stomach was in knots. It was just too much to explain. Bill came in. "Has he moved much today? Looks like he got a haircut."

"Yes, they had to shave him. All of his fur is in a bag."

"So, what's the plan? When does he leave?"

Leave? I had forgotten that plan. I hadn't even talked to the Chinese Crested Rescue contact Carol gave me at the auction.

"Um, they're trying to find a foster home for him." I was lying. But it was feasible that they would be looking for a foster home. Foster homes were so hard to come by.

"I hope it's soon!" Bill's words were genuine, but they hurt me, and I knew he didn't mean to—he had no way of knowing the pain I was coping with after seeing the dogs at the auction. It was a feeling I couldn't shake.

I cried. Uncontrollable tears streamed down my face. I felt total loss. I was exhausted.

"Honey, what is it?" Bill leaned towards me, naïve and helpless.

"You just don't understand. How can you? It was so awful—more than I can fathom," I said, gasping for air.

I sobbed hysterically. I'd held it in so long.

"It's just so much and Thorp is so broken." Words were coming out of my mouth faster than I could process them.

"You named him?" Bill was displeased.

"Yes, I named him." My reaction came from deep inside. "I named him, and I think he has a story to tell. I've never felt surer about anything," I raged.

". . . Or more lost," I thought to myself.

"You need to breathe, relax. Thorp will be OK," Bill said as he held me up.

"It's not just Thorp. You didn't see what I did. You didn't see all of them. Hundreds of them. All broken—their souls empty. Dogs sitting in cages, silent. They were sick and scared. It was cruel."

I sobbed more. I wanted to run out into the streets and scream. Just scream so people got it. They needed to get it.

Bill held onto me tightly. I knew he was at a loss for words. For years, he had seen me bring in strays, nurture sick wildlife, foster pregnant cats. He got me, but I couldn't help wondering if he got this. This was bigger than me. Bigger than us. I had no idea how we were going to fix it.

CHAPTER 6

THE VET

After another sleepless night, I woke up groggy. The emotional toll was becoming a lot for me. I would toss and turn, becoming overwhelmed by the images from the auction: the wire cages haunted me, the putrid smell wouldn't leave my senses, and the empty eyes of the dogs still pierced my soul. I felt guilty for lying in a warm bed and taking such comfort for granted.

Buddy and Sadie were nestled by my feet, and the sight of them brought tears to my eyes. It was so painful to wake to reality: the haves and the have-nots.

Buddy and Sadie weren't always so fortunate.

Buddy's life started in a drug house where he was abused and neglected until his owner died of a drug overdose, and the landlord called animal control. Buddy was then adopted by two nice women, but when they relocated to a small apartment in the city, they no longer had the space to care for him. We adopted Buddy when he was five. He looks a lot like

Benji. Some combination of sheepdog, Wheaton terrier and maybe German shepherd, with a fluffy golden-brown coat.

Sadie actually looks like Benji's girlfriend, Tiffany. A Westie-Maltese-Lhasa mix, all white and silky, she was found as a stray in Columbia, Missouri. Brought to the county animal control, she failed the temperament test for biting. Fortunate to be rescued by Columbia Second Chance, she was fostered and her bio put on Petfinder.com, where I saw her. Within days, I was making the sixteen-hour trek to get her.

I will never forget our car ride home. She sat on my lap the instant that I got in the car. Halfway home, I decided I couldn't complete the full sixteen-hour trip, so we stayed in a random hotel. There, with a dog I'd known only four hours, I slept with her at my side throughout the night.

Even today, Sadie nips at strangers, but we manage her behavior and love her all the same.

I took a deep breath and rose from the shelter of my bed. Planning my next steps down to the laundry room to face the challenges that came with my newly rescued mill dog. It was his day to see my vet.

Thorp was lying on the blanket and stood slowly to greet me. We went outside, and he flailed on the leash but eventually did his business. He'd eaten a small amount of food. In the grand scheme of things, we were making progress.

I coaxed him into my arms, where he stiffened up, his spindly legs awkwardly clinging to my elbows. He began to shake, but then sat unflinching in the front seat of the car.

When we entered the vet's office, I saw all kinds of dogs: some big, some small, some purebreds, some mixes. It was only two days ago that I was standing in an Amish pole barn among hundreds of dogs who had no real families. Hell, they didn't even have names—just cattle tags.

When they asked for Thorp's name, I stumbled.

"Oh, he is so sweet," the receptionist said, smiling.

But all I wanted to do was yell about where he was from and describe the horror that I had seen. The pain and anger I felt was overpowering. It was hard to put it all together and make sense of it. I fumbled for words and said something like, "I just rescued him from an Amish dog auction in Wisconsin."

"Oh, how nice." She smiled again.

And then, I needed to scream. There wasn't anything nice about it. Didn't anyone get it?

I filled out a history report, leaving most of it blank. Because of the minimal regulations on dog breeding, I did not have much information on Thorp. I did have a few papers listing prior vaccines. And since he was registered with the American Kennel Club (AKC), I had his birth date, August 3, 2003.

Dr. Fritz saw us. He was very kind and examined Thorp slowly and gently. We talked of puppy mills, and Dr. Fritz seemed to understand. Finally, someone I could talk to.

Thorp would need dental work. His teeth were badly deteriorated, and he would likely lose many of them: all due to lack of veterinary care and a poor diet. He had a skin infection from all the years of matted fur, and would need further blood work to determine if he had any other infections or diseases.

It was undoubtedly Thorp's first time in a vet clinic in four and a half years.

I paid and gathered Thorp in my arms. His frail body was still stiff and shaking. It had been too much for him. All of the people poking and prodding him. It was ten a.m., and he was shot for the day.

He slept on his bed in the laundry room the rest of the day as I faced the beginning of my battles.

All of my life, I'd had the understanding that if a dog came with AKC papers, it meant the dog was bred by a prominent, responsible breeder. The dog would be healthy, and the lineage of the dog would be sound. If a dog came with AKC papers, it was certain to be of high caliber and, of course, the price of the pup would reflect that.

But in my hand were AKC papers for a sick, matted dog I had bought in an Amish pole barn for sixty dollars. How could I begin to understand?

I was furious. How could the AKC—an organization I believed to be respectable—allow this?

I began my search on the Internet. The AKC website was beautiful. Gorgeous dogs of all breeds. Subheadings with tabs like "Responsible breeding" and "The importance of registering your pups." There was tons of information available, but it wasn't easy to find a way to actually communicate with them. When I finally found a link, I typed:

> I just attended a dog auction in Thorp, WI on March 12th. I ended up rescuing a 4-year-old Chinese crested powder puff–not because of the breed but because it was in the worst shape of any of the dogs there (and that says a lot). This dog came with AKC papers and is known to be from a puppy mill. How on earth can the AKC allow this type of behavior to go on and to continue to allow these cruel people to register their animals? What I saw that day has changed my life. If these are the types of people and the standard of dogs the AKC chooses to support, I believe the AKC has lost all credibility. You can be assured that I will use this dog to demonstrate what AKC really means . . . The general public

needs to know the AKC is in it for
the money and NOT for the
animals!

It was all so unsettling: the images, the Amish, the AKC. My mind couldn't wrap itself around it all, and my heart just kept breaking.

***

In the hours that transpired, I had become quilted into a group of rescuers through so many emails. They were all knowledgeable about what Margie and I called "an underground ring." The stories they told were tragic.

A week ago, I had believed I was a shelter expert. My time at animal control had exposed me to so much (or so I thought), from stray dogs to dog-fighting rings to euthanasia, but nothing had prepared me for the reality of puppy mills.

All I kept thinking was that I'd only been to one dog auction in Thorp, Wisconsin. According to my new friends, there were auctions like this everywhere in the United States. Thousands of dogs on any given day being bought and sold as breeding stock—none with names, only numbers.

After seeing it all, I was still struggling for answers. Sitting in my kitchen, I had nothing concrete to hold onto. I shuffled through the minimal paperwork I had brought to the vet, attempting to piece together all of the craziness.

I wondered if I could trust the rabies vaccination papers that came with Thorp. I posed the question to the experienced group, and they all suggested I should have the vaccination verified by the vet who had administered it. I had the name and phone number of the veterinarian.

I placed the call, and they were happy to verify the information. However, after I reexamined the paperwork, I realized that the vet had seen Thorp on February 28, 2008—only two weeks prior to the auction. If that was correct, that would mean that the vet had to have seen what shape Thorp was in. How could any vet let that go unreported?

It had been a miserable two days, and while I was exhausted, I felt my adrenaline spike. None of this made sense to me, and yet a passion deep inside me yearned to figure it out. Strength I didn't know I had emerged, and I was back on the phone contacting the clinic.

I explained that I had looked at the certificate and noticed the vet had just seen the animal two weeks ago; I said I couldn't help but wonder why on earth he didn't do anything to help him. The receptionist paused and said she wasn't sure who saw the dog. She transferred me to another receptionist. When I repeated my concern, this receptionist asked for my name and said she would get the vet.

I took a deep breath and cleared my throat, unsure what exactly would come out of my mouth. I introduced myself to the vet and said that I'd just attended a dog auction in Thorp, Wisconsin on Wednesday, March 12, and noticed that the dog I rescued was vaccinated by him on February 28, only two weeks earlier.

I knew I was rambling, but I finally found the words to ask how he could vaccinate a dog in such condition and not do anything more to help him.

He began by acknowledging that he knew the dog, but wasn't sure I understood that the dog's owner was Amish.

I knew all too well that the owner was Amish, along with the other hundred Amish and Mennonites who had dogs at the auction.

He further explained how he travels very far to the Amish farms and reminded me that the Amish don't use electricity, attempting to justify vaccinating the dog in the dark.

I couldn't imagine him vaccinating Thorp in the dark and not feeling his excessively matted fur or smelling his rancid coat.

He continued, feeling the need to describe the Amish man as very large and in poor health. He seemed to think I might have met the man. He wanted me to understand that since the man was sick, he thought the dog would be "better off" if sold at auction.

I'm not sure what explanation would have eased my irritation, but it was not this.

Angered, my voice became louder, and I said I didn't care about the sick man, I cared about the sick dog. I explained that it made no sense to me, how selling a dog at a puppy-mill auction would provide a better life for the dog.

The auction images flooded my brain. I became enraged and my voice trembled, yet grew stronger. I ranted about how nearly all of the auction audience was composed of millers, and if I hadn't saved the dog, he could have spent his entire life wasting away in that horrible condition.

His reply was quick, explaining how he had worked with the Amish for a long time and wasn't sure I understood how hard life was for them. He attempted to justify his actions by telling me the Amish do the best they can with their dogs, and he tries to help by vaccinating them.

Sure, vaccines were helpful, but the Amish didn't have just a few dogs—they had hundreds. I couldn't grasp how he wasn't seeing the bigger picture. I suggested he spay and neuter their dogs, but I only heard silence on the line.

I wasn't ready to end the conversation; I still had so many questions. I remembered my vet's words from Thorp's exam, stating how he would report a case like Thorp's. I wanted to know why this vet hadn't.

To my further dismay, he explained that the local animal control didn't respond to calls about neglect or cruelty. He said they only responded when a human was bit because they didn't have the funding or the resources to do more.

It was frustrating. So, I dug deeper and asked if he had ever contacted local legislators to improve the laws and increase the funding.

Ironically, it turned out that his father was a Wisconsin legislator. It felt like such a circular conversation. I kept asking questions, and he would provide answers that only left me with more questions, more frustration.

He ended the conversation frustrated, too. Spinning his words, trying to convince me I had no idea what he dealt with on a daily basis or how difficult his job was.

All of his statements were excuses to me. I didn't care about the Amish man's health or the hard life of the Amish community. I cared about Thorp. I cared about the hundreds of other dogs I saw at the auction. I tried hard to make sense of his viewpoint, but I just couldn't understand how he didn't get it. I couldn't accept how content he seemed with the lack of laws protecting animals.

Was my world so sheltered that such realities were unbearably shocking to me, or was Wisconsin so stuck in the past that vets like him believed they were doing the best they could?

I tried to be polite in closing. I hung up the phone in a complete state of disbelief. I was so upset by the conversation. My heart was racing. My body felt flushed. Everything was unimaginable yet, it was staring me right in the face.

With anger and frustration boiling, I decided to search the Internet for his legislator father. Sure enough, I found Dr. J. A. Hines. He was the forty-second district representative in the state of Wisconsin. Ironically, the rep for his son's district. Even more ironic was that according to all the paperwork, Thorp came from a town near our cabin in: Montello, Wisconsin. And to my chagrin, Representative Dr. Hines also represented my district. I was not a resident of Wisconsin, but I did pay property taxes.

I found Dr. Hines's legislative site and e-mailed him the following:

> Dear Representative Hines,
> I just spoke with your son, Steven Hines, as I was inquiring about a dog I rescued from an auction this Wednesday in Thorp, WI. The dog I got for a mere $60.00 is in horrendous shape. His fur was so matted that the groomer was able to remove it in one entire piece. I noticed on the rabies certificate that your son just

examined (or at least vaccinated) this dog on 2/28/08. I am fairly certain as a past vet yourself that you know a dog could not become this way in just two weeks. This dog has not had a decent home or decent care in years. When I explained to your son that I was appalled a vet could examine a dog in this shape and not do anything about it, specifically not even contact a local animal control or humane society, your son told me that in that area not one of the animal control/humane societies would respond unless a person is bit. Is this true? Shouldn't there be more funding to allow them to do their jobs and care for all animals in a humane fashion?

As a legislator and DVM, and I noticed that you have served on an animal-welfare committee, I would value your opinion. I would like to know why the legislation in WI is so slow to do something to stop the growth of these substandard and cruel puppy mills? What proof do you need to realize they need to be shut down? I would greatly appreciate and value your opinion.

Respectfully,
Rebecca Monroe

*I included my contact
information, using my cabin
address.*

It was in moments like those that I found myself on the brink. Everything I knew about the world was questionable—a trip to a dog auction had rapidly changed my life. Nothing was as it had seemed before I went to the auction, and it felt like nothing would ever be the same again. Things would always be tarnished because of the truths I knew. There was no turning back.

As I played out the morning in my head, I heard the familiar words of my vet, Dr. Fritz, who had said, "We don't see things like this around here, but if we did, I would certainly report it. This is owner neglect, pure and simple."

It was as though I had visited a foreign land, far different from the society I lived in. I had never thought of myself as naïve or ignorant to the truths in life, but this glaring one in front of me made me doubt all prior assumptions about the goodness of people.

I felt the need to cuddle Thorp. To apologize for the life he had been forced to live. It was as though a simple gesture on my part could erase the years he had spent suffering. I knew that wasn't true, but it seemed the only solace I could offer him and myself at the time.

I took him outside, and he sniffed and ventured out further than before. There was confidence in his step. It also became obvious that he was a quick learner, because he knew that if he came in from outside and sat on his bed, he would get a treat. And so he did. It was one of the first times he took the Milk-Bone and actually ate it in front of me.

Thoughts of him becoming an agility dog and competing in jumps and tunnels danced in my head; or possibly, he could be a therapy dog, helping people. In two days, a dog had gone from being a number to being an inspiration. I knew it was only the beginning for #171 and me.

CHAPTER 7

SPOILED

My nine-year-old daughter, Abby, had been at her dad's house since the auction, so she hadn't met Thorp until Saturday morning. Since my time working at animal control, random dogs appearing in our home didn't surprise her. When she walked in and saw him hiding in the laundry room, she looked confused.

"Mom, he's scared. Why?"

I was proud of her ability to assess him. "He came from a scary place."

"Why doesn't he have any hair?" Her voice showed sympathy.

"They had to shave it off because no one ever brushed it." I tried to keep things simple, so she could understand.

"Yuck! Like when I don't brush my hair and it gets all tangly?"

I smiled at her comparison. "Yeah, kinda like that."

"I don't mean to be mean, but he looks sick. Do you think he's cold without hair? We should get him a sweater. I think he would like that."

I was thankful she was so compassionate towards him.

She was eager to go get Thorp a sweater, so we left the house and went to PetSmart. Thorp stayed home. Until we knew his blood-test results, we couldn't expose him to other animals, and it would have been a lot for him to take in. Even our laundry room seemed overwhelming to him at times.

As we browsed the aisles, we saw all types of dogs wagging their tails, following their owners around the store. I couldn't help but be painfully aware of all the unnecessary stuff. The varieties of food, beds, blankets, toys, chews. Deep inside, all I could think about were the dogs at the auction. They would never see a blanket, or a chew toy. Some would never see a full bowl of food or clean water.

The auction had quickly changed my thinking on a lot of things. There were lucky dogs, and then there were mill dogs.

Like on most Saturdays at PetSmart, there was a shelter present with a few adoptable dogs and cats. All of them groomed and in clean kennels. The eyes of these animals were alive. The dogs' tails wagged when people approached, and the cats purred for affection. Short bios graced their cages along with blankets and treats. The dogs were in crates, but they were not the dogs I had seen on Wednesday.

Numerous customers stuck their fingers in for a quick touch. I am sure that by the end of the day, a few of them found good homes.

It made me realize how many homeless animals there were. Even after a few years at the county shelter, I was still shocked by the reality. But, after Wednesday, the truth had really hit me: the last thing this nation needed was more breeding.

We found Thorp a cute sweater and T-shirt to protect his naked body. We picked out some canned food since his teeth were bad, and it was hard for him to chew. Abby grabbed a tube of lotion that was supposed to ease the rash from where the matting was so bad, it was actually knotted to his skin.

We got in line to check out. The clerk asked if we had gotten a new dog. Abby was quick to say, "Yes." It was too hard for me to reply. I didn't know how to respond. Saying we got a new dog didn't seem right. It wasn't the way anyone else got a new dog. This was different. He came from a place no one at the store ever saw. He had lived in conditions that were unimaginable. He was at home now, huddled in a corner of the laundry room because he didn't know how to cope with his new life. He came with baggage that was unexplainable to most people. How could I express all of that? I couldn't muster a single word.

When we got in the car, Abby asked, "Mom, why didn't you tell the lady about Thorp?"

I looked at her beautiful blonde hair and the sparkle in her bright blue eyes. She was so innocent, sitting in the backseat. How would I explain a puppy mill to a nine-year- old? Maybe some parents wouldn't expose their children to such a harsh reality. I wasn't that parent.

"Honey, Thorp came from a puppy-mill auction."

"Yeah, I know. Dad told me you were there and that there were lots of doggies. Why didn't you bring more home? Like when we fostered Oscar, who lost all his hair from bugs. I would have helped take care of more."

"I know you would, but it isn't that simple. Remember coming to animal control and seeing all the dogs in runs? Remember how it made you sad to see all of those dogs needing homes?"

"Yes."

"Well, the auction made me even sadder than that. All of the dogs there were sad, too. None of them ever had a family to love. They were just stacked like shoe boxes in a barn."

I didn't want to cry. I didn't want to scare her. I tried to quickly wipe away the tears, but she saw them.

"Mom, it's bad what you saw, isn't it?"

"Yes." I took a deep breath. It caught me off guard. A nine-year-old understood more than anyone else I had talked to.

"But Mom, you can be happy now. We have Thorp, and he has us to love him and a new sweater to keep him warm."

I smiled. She was right. We did have Thorp and he had us. It just wasn't enough for me.

The moment we got home, Abby was dressing Thorp in his new sweater. He was completely unsure what she was doing, but he sat still for her. When she was finished, he sprang to his feet and seemed to prance around on the tile. He actually seemed proud to have it on. Like, "Wow, look at me. Somebody loves me."

That night, we had a St. Patrick's Day party at a friend's house to attend. I wouldn't have admitted this to anyone, but I was feeling guilty about leaving my little guy. I was never that way with Abby. I always felt she was in good hands with her grandparents, but leaving this guy to go to a party seemed selfish.

Carol Sumbry, one of the wonderful rescuers I had met at the auction, told me that it was important NOT to coddle mill dogs. They needed to realize they couldn't be with you all of the time. She said, "Everyone wants to try and make up for what these dogs have been through. But you can't. Dogs live in the present, and today is what they know. You need to treat them like you do the other dogs if you want them to be stable, healthy animals."

I was grateful for her. She had given me so many tips on what to do with Thorp those first days. Taking in a mill dog was unlike any experience I knew.

Nonetheless, I felt bad for leaving him. I packed the camera so I could show Thorp to my friends and tell them the story of the auction. I was sure it wasn't what they had in mind for a night of celebration. But it was all I had on mine.

Moments after arriving at the party, I had the camera out and was showing my Thorp to anyone who would look. They oohed and aahed, but I could tell they didn't get it.

The conversations were all the same. They would begin, "You got him at an auction? I didn't know there were dog auctions."

"Well, they're puppy-mill auctions. All of the breeders are there to sell their stock or puppies they don't want."

"Oh, were there pugs there? I love that breed."

"Yes, there were lots of different breeds there. Mostly the popular small dog breeds," I said, trying to hold back my frustration.

"I bet they're all so cute."

"Well, actually, most of them are dirty and sick and very scared." It was nearly impossible for me to talk about it.

"Why?"

"Well, puppy mills are mass breeding operations. These people have hundreds of dogs in a barn, and all they do is breed them again and again and sell the puppies to brokers, who then sell them to pet stores. The female dogs are basically bred until they die."

"Oh, that is so sad. We were just talking about getting a dog."

The subject would slowly change. I think they wanted to understand. But it was too hard to picture what was hard to fathom. It was hard for them to believe something so awful actually exists. I knew some of the people at the party had gotten their dogs at a pet store. It hit me—all of the ignorance. The terrible puppy mills existed because too few people knew the truth. I believed that if they saw what I had, they would want to change it. After just a few overwhelming days, I could feel telling the truth was what mattered to me . . . more than anything else.

The night was full of laughter and good times. But for me, it was painful. I could feel the heaviness in my heart—a yearning to make things better than they were. Celebration seemed unsettling after the life-altering four days I had experienced.

CHAPTER 8

FAMILY

Thorp woke up before anyone else. We had gotten home late from the party, and I didn't want him to wake everyone up, so I went downstairs and took him outside. He pottied right away. I wasn't ready to bring him to our bedroom, so I brought him into the family room and placed him on my lap. I was hoping to be able to get more sleep while cuddling him on the couch.

We had gotten a message from the vet that Thorp's blood work came back negative. Luckily, it didn't appear that he had any serious illnesses, which meant he could meet our family pets.

Thorp began to tremble and shake. The family room was a new environment. One of the cats, Sampson, walked in and stood with his front legs on the couch, staring at Thorp. Thorp jerked his head back and shook some more. Two of our other cats, Delilah and Martha, stopped by for a glance.

Thorp didn't understand. He pressed up against me and shuddered. I tried to calm him with my soft voice and gentle massaging touch. There was too much stimulation for him.

He finally lay down in my lap for a few moments, but soon he was back up again, pacing the couch, watching the cats who were lounging around on the floor. They certainly weren't affected by the presence of another dog in the house.

It was obvious Thorp wasn't going to lie down and nap with me. Instead, we sat together and tried to figure things out. I talked to him and told him who all the cats were, and he shook. Once in a while, he would stop shaking and seemed to relax until he heard another new noise.

I continued to pet him until I fell asleep. He must have finally settled down, curled around the backs of my legs, until my husband came down to make coffee.

With Bill came Sadie and Buddy. The dogs charged us. They were bound to figure out who the new guy was on the couch. Sadie came first and sniffed Thorp. Her tail was wagging and she was gentle. It was as if she could smell a combination of his fear and his past. She knew to be nice.

Buddy, who was always a grouch and demanded to be top dog, didn't seem to cater to Thorp's past. Instead, he sniffed him up and down, let out a growl as if to say, "I am in charge around here," and walked away.

Thorp didn't make a sound; he didn't even move. He just shook. It seemed shaking was his only coping mechanism. He curled up tight in my lap and didn't want to move.

Bill made the weekend breakfast: eggs, bacon and toast. He had been a bit perturbed about Thorp coming home with me. But when he said there were some eggs left over and he would scramble them for the dogs, I had a feeling he was including Thorp. Sure enough, moments later, he was equally dishing out eggs to all three bowls. In my heart, I knew he too had found a place for Thorp.

It was a lazy Sunday for all of us. I was drained. The day was cloudy and still cold. There were lots of TV shows to interest us: golf in Orlando with Tiger Woods; the NASCAR race at Bristol; and my alma mater, the University of Illinois, was playing the University of Wisconsin for the Big Ten Championship in basketball. It was definitely a couch-potato day.

Thorp had settled into the chair with me, and the TV watching began. He had stopped shaking and was breathing at a rhythmic pace. I dozed off quite a bit that day, and each time I woke, Thorp was sound asleep. I would stare at him in awe. I felt like it had to be the first time he had truly slept in all his life. He was on a soft pillow, surrounded by a family, safe and warm with a full belly. He was home—something he'd never had before.

Staring at him would bring tears to my eyes because it would remind me what his old life had been like. I thought about the first four and a half years of his life. Born into some breeding home or puppy mill, he was transferred at least once into a miller's hands. There he sat in a chicken-wire cage for endless days and nights. No blankets, no warmth, maybe no light (according to Dr. Hines). His fur became matted, and no one took time to groom him. Once in a while, he was taken out to breed and then stuck back in his cage. Those short moments were all he knew of human touch.

Who knew how many auctions he might have been to? Even if no one ever hit him, he led a life of neglect and emotional cruelty. I would wipe my tears and hold him close to my heart. How I wished I could erase the past.

During one of the TV shows, Sampson jumped on the chair with Thorp and me and snuggled up close to both of us. Sampson is a very large brown tiger cat I rescued from animal control. He had come into the shelter with an eye infection, and due to inadequate treatment (they sewed a button on his eye to hold up the third eyelid), he almost lost his vision and his entire eyeball.

He was the best cat I ever met while working at the shelter, so I took him home one night and brought him to an animal ophthalmologist. There, they were able to remove the button, and with proper medication, they saved his eye. He is a wonderful cat, with a personality as big as his belly.

Sampson wishes he were a dog. He goes to the door when they do, he follows them around the house, and he even eats and drinks from their bowls. So, when he jumped on the chair to join me and Thorp, I knew he just wanted to belong.

It wasn't long before he was cleaning Thorp from head to toe. Thorp appeared comforted by it, and just kept his eyes closed and continued to rest. It was the first time in days when everything seemed right with the world.

When I looked at Thorp, I saw this beautiful, sweet face with an amazing old soul. He wanted nothing more than to feel safe and loved.

He tried a few new things on Sunday. He tried the stairs, but was too scared to go up them. He tried to understand Buddy. But any time he made contact, Buddy would begin to growl or bark, and Thorp would retreat to the laundry room and lie on his little rug.

The laundry room had become his safe zone. We had borrowed a large crate from my friend Ellen, but he wanted nothing to do with it. He would go in if I did, but wouldn't try it otherwise. I left his bed and some rugs and blankets outside the crate. I imagined that to him, a crate was a painful reminder of the life he had left.

CHAPTER 9

AKC

Being on a leash remained a bit of a struggle for Thorp to understand. He didn't pull, but he also didn't walk. If I encouraged him enough, he would eventually walk. But it was very difficult to predict where he would go next.

According to what I read on fostering mill dogs, it was important not to tug at their necks because that was how the Amish grabbed them out of cages.

It was a struggle—coming to terms with it all and then looking into Thorp's eyes. He depended on me. When I washed the floors on my hands and knees, he tried to sit on my lap. He always needed to be close to me. I had become his security.

I would try to cuddle him for a while but then let him down and continue my chores. He was finding new places to "be." The laundry room remained his safety net, but the sofa became a close second. Anything outside of the laundry and family room made him shake.

For the first time, Thorp went outside with Buddy and Sadie. As the two of them ran through the yard, Thorp sat and watched intently. It seemed like he was amazed at the freedom they had.

All of it began to click for Thorp as he watched each of them go to the bathroom, and then he followed. The other dogs were examples for him. On his own, it didn't make sense—the idea of going outside on the grass, the fresh air. He had never had a place larger than two feet square to live in. Now his boundaries were almost limitless, and he had no idea what to do with it all. Seeing Buddy and Sadie, it was as though he realized for the first time he was a dog and no longer somebody's property, or worse, just a product to be bought and sold.

In between household chores and caring for Thorp, I was exercising my American freedom to communicate about the horrors of puppy mills. My latest correspondence was from the American Kennel Club (AKC), in response to my earlier communication with them:

> Hello Rebecca,
>
> Thank you for contacting the American Kennel Club (AKC(r)). It is legal in the United States for anyone to breed dogs and sell them for profit.
>
> The AKC's part in this is to inspect the records and the kennels

of the breeders who breed AKC-registered dogs. The AKC Inspections and Investigations Unit performs almost 5000 inspections a year. When unsafe or unsanitary conditions are discovered in the course of an inspection, the breeder is reported to the authorities who have the power to close down a breeding operation. The AKC does not have the authority to do this. We will suspend a breeder of their AKC registration privileges if he/she is convicted of cruelty to animals. We also will suspend breeders for major violations of AKC Rules and Regulations.

We are doing everything we can, within the legal boundaries, to promote and protect purebred dogs. If you feel that a kennel does not meet acceptable health standards and you want to let us know, we advise that you put your information in writing and send it to:

American Kennel Club
Attn: Investigations & Inspections
5580 Centerview Drive
Raleigh, NC 27606-3390
Phone: (919) 816-3552

I was appalled by their reply on many levels. They chose to not even recognize the term "puppy mill," as if their ignorance proved them innocent. They used "legal boundaries" to hide from their own responsibilities. And they admitted that they would only suspend a license if the breeder was actually convicted by law. After years in animal control, I knew an actual conviction for animal cruelty was often impossible to obtain. If the AKC would stop just taking money from these organizations and allowing anyone to register their dogs as AKC, these puppy mills would be shut down. To me, it was black and white. I replied:

> Thank you for the reply – I appreciate your time. I will be putting in writing the name and address of the puppy mill my Chinese crested powder puff came from as it is obviously a deplorable place which should be shut down.
>
> I can respect that the AKC does not hold the power to shut a place down; however, if the AKC is to maintain any type of standard, I would hope that you have some type of control over who you issue certificates to. The Chinese crested powder puff I saved, while

registered with papers, certainly does not fit the breed standard.

I am curious if you would expound upon what the AKC might be doing to help stop these horrid places called puppy mills, if anything at all. I have to believe that if these places were denied AKC registration, they would be greatly deterred from doing business. The ignorant public seems to think good dogs come with papers. Those of us who are out saving the lives of these so-called purebreds know that their temperament is anything but pleasing to an average family.

As I stated, I will be reporting the puppy mill owner where my dog came from, and if possible, I will get the names and addresses of the breeders of the 250 other dogs that were at the auction on Wednesday. I believe at least 200 of them "came with AKC papers."

I have to admit to you that the AKC appears to have a bad reputation when it comes to ending puppy mills. Rescue organizations are very disappointed in the efforts (or lack thereof) the AKC has taken to help end the misery of so many purebred dogs. I guess I was naive enough to believe the AKC cared about the canine population. I am still holding out hope that perhaps the organization is actually doing something proactive and will prove me wrong.

I will be waiting to hear.

Thank you,

Rebecca Monroe

To the average American, AKC papers represent "best in breed." People pay more for dogs who "come with papers." But here was the truth, right in front of me: the AKC had no real standards. ANY breeder could register a dog and its litter. By submitting some basic paperwork and about fifty dollars, any dog could be AKC.

In just a week, what I knew about dogs and animal welfare had crumbled down around me. I felt blindsided by the grim reality.

Margie and I spent a lot of time talking on the phone, trying to understand the problem.

"Margie, I just don't get it. The AKC acted like it was no big deal. The vet was so nonchalant. What is it that we aren't getting? How can this be happening?" I was so frustrated.

"I know. It's all crazy. Do you think it's all just so underground and all the breeders are in cahoots? Maybe not enough people have actually seen it? I mean, we didn't even know it was going on."

"It's like the novel, *The Pelican Brief.* I feel like we're the people who discover the truth, and we start uncovering all of the players. It feels so dirty, so illegal, so hidden. I actually feel like if we dug too deep, something would happen to us. It's like a nightmare where I can't scream loud enough and I can't wake up and have it be over." The words that came out of my mouth sounded dramatic, but it was the best way to describe how I felt.

"I can't stop thinking about it," Margie said.

"Me neither." Our last words for the day.

A week ago, we were innocent, caring animal lovers, and now I felt like I was compelled to personally stop the horror. In a short time, I had become obsessed with it.

Thorp began to shake less and become more stable in his environment just as I became unstable in mine.

On many levels, I was struggling. Emotionally, I was exhausted. The tears were always waiting to flow at any moment. I was on the edge, balancing all of my raw emotion and the normalcy of my everyday life. Physically, I was frozen. My adrenaline was playing havoc on my body. There were so many ups and downs each day. I had a family to take care of, but I couldn't hold back my desire to fight for the truth.

There were so many atrocities in the world. There was plenty to fix, but for me, the concept of puppy mills was one that should have been easy. I felt like as a society we were regressed a hundred years, and those who could make a difference kept looking the other way.

There were legislators and profitable organizations, like the AKC, who could end all of the cruelty. I was left wondering why they hadn't.

Universal health care, war in Iraq, Social Security reform, national education—these were the issues that plagued our country, due to their vastness and the complexities involved to fix them.

There were no complexities when it came to puppy mills. There were good people and there were bad people. The bad people represented themselves without camouflage for anyone willing to look and to see. They had cages upon cages stacked in barns without heat, without light. Their animals were matted and not vaccinated. Their dogs looked with blank stares and empty eyes.

These places were as identifiable as road signs and green grass. Right in front of our eyes, they existed. Waiting for the right inspector, the right legislator, and the right business to say enough is enough.

I went to bed at night a different person. I used to worry about my tomorrow: what errands I had to run, what room needed to be cleaned and what friend I needed to get back to. Those thoughts were replaced with ones of puppy mills. My mind was full of the vividness of the auction, the souls of the dogs I knew no one could take that day, the words of the heartless Amish looking only for "the best ones," and the horrible truth that, sadly, I had only seen a fraction of the reality.

CHAPTER 10

MOMENTS

When Thorp, Buddy and Sadie went out for the morning stroll, I noticed that Thorp sniffed too. He wasn't as concerned about the leash, or me, or even the chill on his naked body. He was sniffing the ground like a "real" dog.

Dogs should sniff. They should enjoy the outside. Perhaps the human race needs to enjoy the moment more often in order to stop and look at the society we've created.

We need to allow dogs to teach us about the present, the very moment we are living in. When dogs go for a walk, they aren't in a hurry to get done and get on to the next "to do" on their list. They are relishing the moment. They appreciate each step, each tree and each smell. For them, it is about nothing else but the present.

Thorp revels in the moment. He rolls on his back on the sofa and wiggles and stretches out. He enjoys the fact that he is no longer on chicken wire. He is in a warm home. He gulps his food as he gets it because he doesn't know if more is coming. He snuggles in my lap because he can.

Whether dogs are able to remember is something I leave to the scientists. What I do know is that Thorp doesn't hold me responsible for what happened to him. He doesn't dwell on the pain and anguish he experienced his first four years of life. Instead, he lives for the day.

Perhaps it is the little moments in life we take for granted that numb us to the indifference in the world.

After the auction, I could finally see the indifference around me. People with so much to be thankful for, yet still not embracing true joy, and too busy to care about making a positive impact on the world around them. It was a devastating realization for me. And I was just as guilty.

I was blessed to find #171 because it was the beginning of something huge in my life. I knew there was a story to tell and a sad, pathetic dog would be the one to help me tell it. What I didn't know is that along the way, in just a few short days, he would have such an impact on my own life and all the moments that would follow . . . forever.

CHAPTER 11

A WEEK

I woke up to Thorp barking in the laundry room. He was barking! Had he found his voice? I went down, said good morning and took him outside.

It was only 5:30 a.m., so I took him back up to bed with me. Buddy and Sadie were sleeping in Abby's room. None of them would be up for another hour.

I placed Thorp in my bed, and he immediately started rolling around on his back. He was stretching and rubbing. It was as though he knew this was the good life. Being groggy, I snuggled back under the covers and hoped Thorp would eventually follow suit.

He did. He curled up against the outline of my body and took a deep sigh. Instantly, I realized it was a week ago we had found each other and both our lives had changed beyond belief.

I whispered to him, "It's been a week, Thorp. You had no idea where you were going to end up when you sat at that auction, and here you are."

Really, neither of us had known what to expect a week ago. We both entered that barn unaware of how that day would affect our entire lives.

One week. It was amazing what could happen in a week. I had encountered one of my greatest fears: the reality of puppy mills. I had taken on a vet, a legislator and the AKC. I had written a story that would change everything.

Some people might have been able to go to that auction and go back to their lives unchanged. Somehow, for some reason, that was not possible for me. I felt like a survivor, and nothing I knew would ever be the same.

The effects of the auction were staying with me. There didn't seem to be a minute when I wasn't reminded of the emptiness of that day. I was at a turning point—a breaking point for me. A pivotal moment that both broke my heart and fed my soul.

The personal realization: puppy mills gave me purpose. The tears I shed proved to be fuel for battling forward. Making sense of it all meant facing my own fears, as complex as cruelty and as simple as public speaking. My writing was shaping others' perceptions—my voice was quietly being heard. It had only been seven days.

CHAPTER 12

FRESH START

It was nothing short of miraculous: Thorp sprang to his feet and ran around the house like a puppy. He was pure and frisky and I could sense his glee. He even took Sadie Mae's bunny toy and threw it in the air. He wanted to play.

That is until grumpy old Buddy growled and towered over him. Thorp was too new to the household and too scared to stand up to him.

It was rewarding to see Thorp happy. Genuinely happy. It became obvious that living with other dogs was essential to a puppy-mill dog's adaptation to a normal life. Thorp thrived on watching Buddy and Sadie and figuring out what he was supposed to do. (The good and the bad habits!)

Thorp always found a way to snuggle into my lap. Didn't matter what I was doing, he always got in there and rested his head. The fact that Thorp wanted to sit in my lap was confirmation that he had never belonged in a chicken-wire cage. He yearned for human contact.

Even after four and a half years of seclusion, it was all he wanted.

It was affirmation that puppy mills are not humane. They go against the very nature of these loyal animals, and the unconditional love they give to us.

I was amazed at how easily they forgive. I know I was not the one who tortured Thorp, but it's unbelievable that he knows it, too. Humans don't forgive that easily. We seem to make everyone pay for someone else's wrong to us.

If we were ever to really slow down and pay attention, we would see just how much there is to learn from our pets. The same animals we are so quick to hurt, use or throw away are the same animals who offer us love without limits, loyalty without boundaries and their own lives without expectations.

***

The day had come for Thorp to be neutered and to have his teeth cleaned. I was scared for him. I trusted my vet, often saying that I would rather go to him than my own doctor, but leaving Thorp for the day to have surgery felt like betrayal. All the trust I had earned from him would be lost. I didn't want him to think I was abandoning him, something he knew all too well in his life.

Knowing about Thorp's previous life of neglect made me highly sensitive to him. It was as though I could erase all of the bad he had suffered, if I could just make everything right today.

Thorp's teeth were in bad shape. It was likely that some of his teeth would have to be removed because of the decay. He had spent too many years with no vet care and a poor diet. The health of canine teeth was critical to the rest of their overall condition.

As with every visit to the vet, the tech came out and sat with me in the lobby.

"Is this Thorp?" the tech asked.

"Yes," I said nervously.

"Great. So, a basic neuter and teeth cleaning today?"

It was something she had said a hundred times before, but it was the first time Thorp had ever heard such words. In four and a half years, he had never known any veterinarian care. To puppy-mill dogs, vet care doesn't exist.

"Yes, that's it for him. I think there's a good chance he'll have some teeth pulled, according to Dr. Fritz."

"Sure, we'll take a look when we get in there. We'll call if there's anything more serious. Is this a good number to reach you today?"

I nodded, fighting back tears. It wasn't a big deal. I knew that. But handing over Thorp to anyone broke my heart. In just a few weeks, the bond we shared had grown so much. We had found one another in such a grim and terrifying situation, and afterwards, so much changed for both of us. I needed him and he needed me.

Even though he would finally be getting much-needed medical care, it was heart wrenching to watch as the tech took him away to the surgery center. As he disappeared, I caught my breath and left before I could burst into tears.

Later in the day, they called to let me know Thorp was doing well and had had four teeth removed. There was some infection throughout his mouth, but with antibiotics he would be fine. I could get him after five p.m.

I arrived at the vet's at 4:59 p.m. I was anxious to bring him home. I knew he was scared, and I was so afraid he would think I had forgotten him. When the tech brought him out, the first thing I noticed was his eyes. They were looking right at me. My heart melted. His tail wiggled slightly when I said his name. He knew me.

"He's awfully sweet," the tech said.

"Thorpy . . ." My voice trembled. He was groggy and definitely overwhelmed. The tech went over the meds and what to expect for his recovery. I listened as best I could, but my eyes never left Thorp's gaze. Something as mundane as a neuter and as simple as a teeth cleaning, yet to dogs like Thorp, these procedures were rare. Most dogs in mills die of cancer or complications from not being spayed or neutered, or end up with serious infections or heart conditions because of the lack of dental care.

To the vet, it was just another day, but to Thorp, it was a miracle.

I held him close as we walked out together. It was a fresh start for Thorp. I was grateful that he would be fine, but soon it hit me that there were thousands of dogs left untreated in stacked cages all over the country. Dogs who would eventually die with no vet care—without even a name of their own.

CHAPTER 13

EVOLUTION OF TRUTH

I woke up tossing and turning again. I was still overwhelmed by the auction and what I had seen on March 12. I knew it had consumed me. But as I lay awake, I thought about evolution.

All those years of domesticating the wolf so he could become man's best friend, and this is how we've turned on him. We shove him in a tiny wire cage, isolate him from the very people he came to trust, and enslave him to breed until he has but one breath left. Then, without hesitation, we suffocate him and erase his life completely.

It is truly a dichotomy and a betrayal in the highest and lowest of forms. I thought we, as a race, should be ashamed of who we have become and what we allow one another to do.

More and more e-mails kept coming in about the story I had posted on the Best Friends website. People commended me for my courage and my ability to tell it like it is. Most started their e-mails with, "Your story brought me to tears."

I didn't want to make people cry, but I did want them to see what cruelty exists in this world. After they commended the story, they always asked, "What can I do?" For this I, too, was at a loss. I felt like I was only doing half the job by telling the story. There must be more. Breaking the silence of these animals' suffering was not enough.

What could people do? The solution was simple: get rid of puppy mills. Yet, if it were simple, why wasn't it already done? Why did they still exist? Was it a matter of communication and awareness? Was it such an underground operation that the general public didn't have a clue?

It was basic supply and demand.

The puppies Thorp sired went to brokers. Those brokers sold the puppies to pet stores across the country, and some of them might have been sold online.

The obvious answer was to tell people to stop buying puppies from pet stores—even better would be to stop buying anything from stores that sell puppies. The answer seemed simple, but sadly, it wasn't. People really believed that the pups at pet stores came from local breeders when in reality, no responsible breeders would sell their puppies to pet stores. If everyone could just see with their own eyes what I had seen.

I struggled with what to say, so I said, "Share the story—share the truth."

I was sitting on the sofa when Thorp ran into the room. He looked up at me as if to say, "What do you want from me?"

He jumped up on the sofa and kept staring at me. I said to him, "Thorp, this is it. This is how your life was supposed to be all along. All I ask is for you to be a dog. A good dog. Please, no peeing in the house. I can handle just about anything else. This is it, Thorp. All you need to do is be. Play ball, bark at strangers, and lie on the couch. This is how dogs are supposed to live. No wire cages, no dark barns. That part of your life is over, and you will never have to go back."

Those were my words, and yet they formed a lump in my throat. I could say them to Thorp, but I questioned their truth for other dogs because of what I had witnessed. There were many people who didn't feel that way. There were hundreds of dogs at the auction who would never hear those words, let alone live them.

I said those words to Thorp because they came straight from my heart. I knew I wouldn't be able to stop saying them until they were true for all dogs.

Later in the day, when I checked my phone messages, I found I had a call from Representative Doc Hines. He was returning my e-mail and would rather talk than write. My heart raced. I was elated, and a little freaked-out.

I had e-mailed him out of a purely emotional reaction. His son had pissed me off, and that was my response. I was so new to all of it. I had no idea what I would even say to him. Before I could return his call, I had to be fully prepared.

I immediately e-mailed the rescue forum, looking for inside advice. Only one person e-mailed me back. She had a few thoughts, but no one even seemed excited that I had gotten the phone call. I was confused.

I was realizing that there were two sides to everything. I had learned a while back that everyone had their talents and their interests, and rarely did they intermingle. People who come to shelters to clean and care for animals rarely like to do fundraising. It was as though two different volunteer groups were needed to accomplish both tasks.

Now I was finding that there were two types of puppy-mill rescuers: those who do everything to get the dogs out and find them homes, and those who protest and communicate with legislators and officials to get the mills closed.

It was not that one type was better than the other. It was that they didn't each operate on both levels. But that was where I found myself: with Thorp, and communicating with legislators and vets and anyone else I could get to listen.

I had no idea what the hell I was doing, but I just kept going. Sometimes, for a moment or two during the day, I would forget the tragedy, and life would seem normal. Abby would come home from school and Bill from work. To them, it was just another day.

They were growing to like Thorp, though his insecurities and lack of normalcy were completely unbelievable to them.

"Mom, why is he still afraid of things? Will he ever act like Buddy?" Abby was frustrated with such an odd dog.

Bill was still in disbelief that we were keeping him.

"Honey, is he really staying? You couldn't find anyone to take him? I suppose it's hard to find a home for a dog like him. Those are the ones the Monroes get."

They meant well. And while they didn't prevent me from moving forward, I knew talking to them about it was pointless. I had seen something they didn't know existed. They didn't share my experience, so it was hard to relate to me. The truth is, even if they had been there, they still wouldn't have had my fury. They would have been saddened and disgusted, but the fire in my blood was only mine.

I was just one person, but I had to keep fighting.

CHAPTER 14

SHADOWS

Each night, I would put Thorp to bed in the laundry room. He was still having problems with potty training, and the familiar room seemed to provide him with security. He would sleep until five a.m. most days.

One night, he woke up at 11:30 p.m., barking and barking. I got up to let him out. We went outside and walked around the yard. The sky was dark, ominous and gray. The clouds were thick, hazy and hovering low. Behind me, the moonlight struck my back and cast my shadow out into the yard. It was a long, towering shadow, thin and lean in the vastness of the wintering, dormant lawn.

I couldn't help but project the weeks' events onto the scene before me: the largeness of the puppy-mill trade, the looming of the slow and passive legislation, and me—one person—standing alone among it all. I felt the way my shadow looked, surrounded by the darkness of the night.

Just one human being, trying to make sense of it all and trying to make right with the world.

When I came in, I caved and for the first time let Thorp come to bed with me. He curled up against my side, sighed and fell fast asleep.

Later the next morning, I was driving home from town, and snow flurries were blowing through the cold, damp air. I was taken back to the drive home from the auction.

I remembered my heart pounding, my eyes burning and the overall numbness I felt. In the back of the car was this dog I didn't even know.

The drive itself was blacked out from my memory. I think the events of the day overtook me. Five plus hours, and all I remembered was the auction. I remembered the emptiness of the animals, the evil of the millers and the uneasiness of the rescuers. I remembered the passion of the protesters outside and the apparent oblivion of the buyers inside.

I remembered the cold of the pole barn, the thickness in the air, and the eeriness of the day. I remembered the rain, the sleet and the snow outside, and the forgotten protest signs lying in the muddy parking lot.

Though it was spring, the winter prevailed. As the auction did, deep in my soul.

I silently said to myself as I drove, "I am but one, but this one made a difference to Thorp, and I will make a difference to more."

I remembered the imagery from the other night outside, and it struck me: "Shadows are images of light when blocked by something bigger."

That was what this was! There shouldn't be shadows on puppy mills, but there was so much blocking the fight. And there was yet another truth: too many dogs in the United States—and across the world. Millions of unwanted animals are euthanized every year because there are not enough homes for them. Why on earth did we need puppy mills?

I thought if people could realize that AKC papers meant nothing, purebred animals would become a thing of the past. People would understand that the dog at the shelter is just as good a pet as the one who comes with "pure" bloodlines.

I couldn't get past the greed that had overtaken the original intentions of the AKC. They allowed money to tarnish their mission. And in return, it watered down the very essence of their organization. Anyone who wanted a purebred Chinese crested could come and visit Thorp and see for himself that though he was registered, he certainly wasn't a grand champion. Yet he was bred again and again . . . God only knew what his offspring were like.

I was filled with ideas and questions. I felt like I had so many solutions and was naïve enough to think no one else had thought of them before, as if I were the first person to fight for the cause.

I think I felt like that because it made so little sense to me that something so inhumane was still legal.

CHAPTER 15

REALITY

For the first time in weeks, the adrenaline running through me ceased.

I spoke to Dr. Yvonne Bellay, head veterinarian for the state of Wisconsin's Department of Agriculture, and finally spoke to Representative Doc Hines. I talked to Dr. Bellay first, for about forty-five minutes. I could tell she was a wonderful woman who had stuck to the profession for a long time. She was kind and sincere and allowed me to ask her anything. She taught me a lot during our conversation.

For me, puppy mills were a relatively new battle. I had known for some time they were out there. I hadn't bought a dog or cat at a pet store in over thirty years. I grimaced each time I passed a pet store and thought about where those dogs came from, and I knew not to patronize them.

But realistically, my true passion against puppy mills started on March 12 around twelve p.m., when I looked into my first-ever puppy-mill dog's eyes. I remember the first dog I saw, the Maltese, and the long rows of dogs in cages just like hers. I remember being horrified.

That was when the sadness and the rage ignited in me. That was MY moment.

Talking to Dr. Bellay, I was enlightened about Wisconsin's moment. For nine years, Dr. Bellay and others had been working on legislation to end the horrors of the mills. To date, there was not one single regulation governing what they called the pet "industry." It deeply saddened me to hear of dogs considered an industry and not loyal companions.

For nine years, numerous bills had been introduced. Sadly, all of them had failed in some fashion. Much of the time, it was because of underfunded resources to enforce the new proposed laws. The most recent bills, which were introduced in 2008 and fondly coined "the lemon law," were known as SB 308 and AB 567. The premise was that if inadequate breeders were held to replacing any sickly dogs, this would cut into their profits, and eventually it would deter them from breeding altogether.

It also meant that the dog the owner bought would be returned to the breeder—to either be kept for more breeding or euthanized however the breeder saw fit.

Thankfully, those bills fell flat. Since it was an election year, the Wisconsin legislature was out, so no more bills would be introduced.

Dr. Bellay did tell me that a legislator had formed a committee to draft a new bill to propose. I was quite optimistic when she told me who was on the committee: Eilene Ribbens, director of the No Wisconsin Puppy Mill Project; Chuck Wegner, director of the Clark County Humane Society (where I had found out about the auction); Dr. Bellay; and other humane-minded individuals I had heard of. The only black sheep on the committee was Wallace Havens. He was the owner of one of THE largest breeding facilities (aka puppy mills) in the state of Wisconsin. In my mind, he should have been in prison. However, I rationalized that since there were no laws regulating his operations in Wisconsin, he would represent the breeders. If nothing else, perhaps he would bring diversity to the group and potentially buy in from other millers.

Dr. Bellay was also kind enough to explain to me that for all practical purposes, Wisconsin had no system for animal control and humane enforcement. There were no regulations anywhere in the state that mandated having a department, division or even a human being responsible for humane law. With cheap prices for land and farms, it became glaringly obvious why Wisconsin was such a fertile state for puppy mills.

Dr. Bellay expressed her pride in a program they had begun in 1999. They developed a training program where any jurisdiction could appoint a civilian to be a humane officer. This person would be educated, trained and certified in humane law. This program was run through the Department of Agriculture.

It had been a slow process, but she said that she was optimistic about it. As of late, more and more law enforcement officers were appointing themselves for the training, simply because they cared about animal welfare in the state.

I was forced to see the reality in Wisconsin. Puppy mills were just a small piece of what was wrong in the state concerning animal welfare.

It was a lot to digest—to fully acknowledge the shortcomings, and to realize my fight was only one of many just in the state of Wisconsin. I couldn't begin to comprehend what the situation was nationally.

I waited a few hours as I grappled with what I knew and managed to tame my nerves. Later in the day, I found the courage to return Representative Doc Hines's call. I was nervous. I had never approached a legislator personally about a topic I was so passionate about. Not to mention, I had already attacked his son in my e-mail.

From the get-go, I could tell that Representative Hines, or "Doc" as he preferred to be called, was a rather laid-back politician. He had followed his professional career as a veterinarian and somehow ended up in politics.

Right away, there was an easy tone to our conversation, and I felt more relaxed. I didn't want to fight or scream. I wanted to learn and understand.

He repeated, in his own way, many of the things Dr. Bellay had spoken to me about. Only, as a politician, he emphasized all the things he had attempted to do.

Three years ago, he put forth a bill, AB 536, which he felt mirrored a successful one that Colorado had adopted. He said it was struck down because those who would enforce the bill felt there weren't enough resources attached to it. He told me that it included one full-time vet and a part-time support person.

I was not versed in government or even aware of how big the state of Wisconsin was . . . but I could agree that one vet and one support person couldn't manage the ENTIRE state of Wisconsin and the puppy-mill epidemic. But at least he had tried something.

He expressed to me his view of the nature of the people of Wisconsin. The state maintains a farm mentality, and within that mentality came many roadblocks to passing humane legislation. He said many people were opposed to doing anything at all about the puppy mills.

Actually, I could relate to the farm mentality in Wisconsin. For five years, I had worked in Clinton, Wisconsin, as a human resource professional. I spent a lot of time with many men and some women who had grown up on farms. For the most part, these were the people I hired to work in our manufacturing plant. They had an outstanding work ethic and were always willing to work long, hard hours because they were used to it on the farm.

In those five years, I also learned a lot about the farm mentality. Though many of these people loved their dogs and cats, they were just animals to them. Paying for vet services and grooming was not how they would choose to spend their hard-earned money.

However, there was one dramatic difference between these people's farm mentality and the mentality of the millers: farmers respected their animals because they knew these animals ultimately provided their livelihood.

Somehow, that was something that did not translate to the puppy-mill industry. I believed that even the people I had once worked with, who came from farms, would be appalled to see how these dogs were treated.

He brought up my concern about his son's performance with Thorp. He explained that there were no laws requiring a vet to report cruelty or neglect to the authorities.

I told him that I understood that now. But, I asked, "As a vet, not a legislator, do you have issues with what your son did?"

He said of course he did.

That was all I really wanted: confirmation that above any legal demand was individual responsibility.

Representative Hines and I discussed the lack of humane law enforcement in the state, and he seemed to be OK with that. I could tell that we certainly weren't going to change much with our conversation.

He was amicable, and he listened to what I had to say, but we came from different sides of the coin.

The entire conversation was summed up for me when I asked what programs the rabies registration dollars funded in the state of Wisconsin. In my county, that money went directly to our animal-control budgets and helped to fund animal-control expenses, including humane education, animal welfare and adoption.

Representative Hines said, "Well, that money has always been earmarked for dog damages."

Before I could ask what those were, he continued and said, "Anytime someone's livestock was damaged by roaming dogs, they were supposed to be able to collect their financial losses from the rabies registration money."

I gulped. It seemed such an antiquated issue.

He continued to explain that they had found not all the counties were using that money for its original intended purposes and instead were giving it to humane societies.

He quickly pointed out that he had introduced legislation, which regulated that 25 percent of all rabies tag money would be set aside until the end of the year for dog damages. If none were incurred or the money wasn't all used up, then it could go towards whatever the county desired.

In disbelief, I thanked Representative Hines for his time and hung up the phone.

It seemed a travesty to me that money obtained through animal fees was not utilized to protect and propagate humane education. Once I heard that, I knew ending puppy mills represented only a fraction of the work to be done in Wisconsin.

And with that, I found myself searching within on where to go next. I felt like I had exhausted all of my individual resources. Should I join up with No Wisconsin Puppy Mills? Was my news story enough? Should I just be satisfied with that? I felt as though I had come to the base of a hill I thought I could climb, only to find that a cloud was covering the peak, and now when I looked up, I saw an entire mountain range.

Could I still make the climb?

CHAPTER 16

SHAKEN

Life with Thorp had settled into a daily pace. The ranting phone calls, the adrenaline rush, the tears—all of it had taken a quiet break. I think my body needed it. I was on the verge of a breakdown of sorts. I knew that there were worse plights in life than seeing a dog auction firsthand, but for me, it had become the core of my existence.

The more soul-searching I did, the more convinced I became that my life had prepared me for all of it. Everything that had led up to this fight seemed to make sense.

I had always stopped for every stray on the road and took it home or to a shelter. I had always wanted to do more for animals. Some, including my mother, had thought I was cold because my empathy wasn't as easily spent on human beings. I always felt a stronger compassion for animals. I think it's because I saw them as so helpless, so innocent. I always believed that if I didn't help them, no one else would.

I had spent years harboring animals of all kinds: dogs, cats, birds, frogs, caterpillars. My passion was biased: animals first. If a creature needed help, I was there.

One summer, growing up on the lake, a white domestic goose found its way to our dock. His head had been disfigured—we assumed from a motorboat accident. He spent months recovering in our yard, using his beak to knock on the door when he was hungry, or sunning himself on the pier. One day, he swam away and never came back. We called him "Happy."

There was the summer of sophomore year, when my best friend, Kelly, and I rehabbed a sparrow. Five straight days of around-the-clock feedings every fifteen minutes until the day he flapped his wings and flew away.

I had single-handedly treated a dog for sarcoptic mange. Oscar came to animal control on a call of neglect. When he arrived, more than half of his fur was gone, and his skin was so scarred he looked like an elephant. For weeks, I bathed Oscar and gave him meds, and eventually his fur started to grow back in patches. He even found a loving home.

I have bottle-fed squirrels and tube-fed possums. I have fed cougars and walked foxes.

Everything I had done, all of the animals I had saved, had brought me to the journey I was on. Each of them had given me more strength, more experience to keep going.

So, when I was faced with one of my worst nightmares—numerous, helpless animals, all broken in spirit—my entire view of the world was shaken. I had known such cruelty existed, but seeing it with my own eyes and having it reach into my soul was more than eye-opening—it was life-changing.

CHAPTER 17

JUDGMENT

Thorp and I went to visit a friend one day. We chatted for two hours, as he sat on either my lap or hers the entire time. He was shaking at first, but gradually became at ease. He was content.

It was in moments like those that I wanted to know what he was thinking. Did he even remember the mill? Watching him in my friend Debbie's lap made me pause and wonder why more wasn't being done to banish mills altogether. Thorp lay in our laps, a sweet and peaceful dog. Why on earth should he ever have been caged like a wild creature?

Over spring break, Debbie's daughter got a turtle. I had suggested a rescue, but they found an exotic pet store in a town close to ours. Debbie knew how I felt about pet stores and made a point of telling me about how nice the store was and that they did have relinquished turtles for adoption. The mere fact that she gave it some thought was a step in the right direction.

Situations like this made me start to realize that the mere presence of Thorp in other people's lives was causing them to think about rescuing animals. Slowly, we were raising awareness.

I was starting to pay close attention to where people got their dogs. I would ask the question with a lump in my throat, waiting for the answer—the term "pet store" broke my heart. I knew all I could do was continue to spread the truth that I had come to know. All I could do was educate people on where pet-store puppies came from and the number of dogs in need of rescue.

Designer dogs were all the rage. Truthfully, "designer dog" was only an in-vogue term for mutt or mixed breed. Designer dogs made up many of the breeds coming in large quantities from the mills. People were paying thousands of dollars to get a teacup "Shih-poo" or "Yorkie-poo." All I saw were the mothers of those dogs, stuck in the barns with little chance of ever being someone's beloved pet.

Driving home from Debbie's, I couldn't help but think about an earlier moment at my vet's office: how it had made me question who I was and wonder who exactly was supportive of puppy mills. When I least expected it, the good in people was reaffirmed.

A man and his teenage son had come into the vet's office with a cat in a carrier. They weren't dressed very nicely, and the man was rather gruff. He had a long beard and the whole Harley Davidson biker facade going on. They were explaining to the receptionist that they had forgotten to take away the cat's food and water after midnight. The man seemed irritated by the whole situation. As wrong as it was of me, I had lowered my expectations of the care the cat was receiving from its owners.

When the vet tech came out to describe the procedure to the man and his son, it was all I could do not to cry. The teenage son took out the cat and held her. He started telling the tech that they had just adopted her from a shelter. He told her what a good cat she was and how much he had already grown to love her.

The once seemingly gruff man had his arm around his son and was telling him not to worry. The man started telling the vet how sorry he was about the food and water. He wanted to know if there was any way to safely proceed with the scheduled surgery. He went on to explain how they had another cat and just didn't think about taking away the food.

The tech assured them it would be OK. They would push back the cat's surgery to later in the day. The teenage boy gave the tech the cat's blanket and then reluctantly handed his cat over to her. Stroking her head to calm her, he mentioned one last thing to the tech: "You know, when we went to pick her out, she was the one who came to me."

The tech promised to take good care of her, and the man and his son left. And I felt like an ass.

I thought about that all day. Besides teaching me the obvious about not judging people, it also made me wonder who was OK with puppy mills. At first glance, I would have assumed that those two men would not care about such things. But I would have been wrong. They had gone out of their way to adopt their cat from a shelter and were now devoted to her. I knew they would care. Why was this fight so hard?

CHAPTER 18

SHAMEFUL NEWS

It had been three weeks since the auction—almost exactly, as it was 12:30 p.m. It had been quite a wild ride. My emotions had been all over the board. I was coming out of the haze and was able to look back, somewhat rationally, at the last three weeks of my life and how it had changed.

I was deleting e-mail when I came across a bunch from Carol Sumbry, the woman I had introduced myself to right before bidding on Thorp. She had e-mailed me often after the auction, yet I didn't remember any of the messages. As I was going through them, I found one that should have helped me through my emotional pain. Unfortunately, I had never read it.

She had written and told me how she had suffered the same type of emotional backlash after going to a farm to rescue puppy-mill dogs. She said for days, she was in a fog. Her husband kept asking her what was wrong, and she finally was able to say, "I am ashamed to be of the human race."

That was it. That was EXACTLY how I felt since attending the auction.

I was ashamed. Ashamed that in a developed country, we allowed something so cruel.

It was never that I didn't think cruelty existed. I knew it did—it was just so hard to accept when it looked me in the eyes. Especially when it felt so unnecessary.

I felt shame because it was so obvious that greed was the reason. The well-being of man's best friend was forsaken in the name of profit.

Knowing that made the world seem so cold, so brutal.

I think I was ashamed of what I had—the luxuries, the comforts; but mostly I was ashamed of being ignorant of a truth so close to my heart. Dogs were being abused by the thousands, and I had led much of my life unaware.

Unbelievably, while I was searching for answers and attempting to share my newfound knowledge with others, Oprah aired her first segment on dogs in puppy mills and shelters. Friends were calling and e-mailing, telling me they were crying their eyes out. It was a very eye-opening episode. I couldn't imagine what the average person felt while watching it.

Oprah went where few people had. A Texas shelter allowed her in the back. They actually euthanized dogs on TV and showed them being placed in body bags and dumped in bunches in the garbage. Even to someone like me, who had seen euthanasia firsthand, it was devastating.

But her show made the critical point: puppies are being churned out in horrendous conditions while good dogs are being killed every day. Her show blatantly made the case for reality—there were already too many dogs.

When I first tuned into the show and watched the puppy-mill undercover investigation, I was screaming inside, "That isn't enough. It's worse than that."

All the dogs they showed were fighting for human attention. I found what I had witnessed more heartbreaking: dogs who ignored people or even tried to avoid them. It meant that their spirits were broken and they had given up. I grappled with that and decided perhaps this was too hard to convey through a television set.

After Oprah, I sent letters to the local papers for the editorial sections. I knew it was important to seize the moment. I wrote:

Regulations for the Pet Industry
To the Editor:

  Thank you to those who were brave enough to watch Oprah Winfrey's segment on puppy mills and shelters, which aired April 4. I am sure it was horrifying to most who were able to endure all the footage. As a person who has seen it all firsthand, I can tell you that none of it was exaggeration. Please, before you wipe your tears and put away the Kleenex, take action. Write to both state and federal legislators and demand that there be stricter regulations on the pet industry. To see animals treated so inhumanely is a sad message about the state of our society. You were brave enough to watch, now be brave enough to make a difference.

Becky Monroe
Woodstock, IL

I also contacted two papers to express my desire for them to do a news story on puppy mills. I explained that Thorp could be the local lead-in, and then they could end by encouraging people to adopt from our great local shelters. It was actually my third attempt at the *Northwest Herald*. I tried a different editor, and all he did was e-mail me back and say he had passed the story on to the news editors. I hadn't heard anything from the *Independent*, another local paper.

It was infuriating. I couldn't help but believe it was the perfect follow-up to Oprah's national show.

A show which earned Oprah THE most success she had ever had on one segment, and yet the papers floundered with the subject.

I was learning the reality of media—the truth was not always what they sought. It made me question their loyalties and intentions. For example, it was common for the *Northwest Herald* to print large, full-page ads for Petland, a known buyer of mill dogs according to Humane Society of the United States (HSUS) investigations. In addition to the full-page ads were numerous daily ads in the classified section, listing the puppies Petland had for sale. It was easy to see the business conflict a story about puppy mills could create.

It was eye-opening—all of it. First, it was the horror of the mills, then the truth of poor legislation, and then even the media fell short of my expectations. It was as though I had been walking around in a bubble for years, assuming the world was an honest place.

CHAPTER 19

EXPLOITATION

One of the members of the Wisconsin rescue forum e-mailed everyone pictures of the Cavalier King Charles pups that were born to a mom they had rescued at the Thorp auction in March. I found it calming to know that those precious pups weren't starting their lives in the horror of the mill. And as the rest of the rescuers replied, I realized it was even more important that the mom, Lola, wasn't giving birth there either.

Shayla Willmarth, the rescuer of Lola, sent me pictures of the hack jobs the Amish had done on cesarean births. She had a picture of a beautiful King Charles named Peony whom she had rescued at a prior auction. Poor Peony had wire stitches: she had been brutally wired shut after a cesarean section. Shayla said that when they auctioned her off, they never even mentioned that she had just given birth. The entire incision looked like a Neanderthal had done it. The rescue vet said the metal wire had been in for over three weeks.

If it was not enough that these animals lived their lives in feces-infested, wire-bottomed cages without any love or human companionship, the mere fact that they were treated like raw meat—cut open and stitched with savage materials—should have been enough to make puppy mills illegal. Each day, I was forced to realize the previously unimaginable exploitation of innocent animals.

I went to bed with the vivid photo of Peony's tender tummy wired shut in my mind. The thought of the pain she had endured, all alone, stabbed at my heart. All I could envision was this sweet little Cavalier King Charles, a breed known for its gentle nature, ripped open by a wild beast, her puppies abducted, and then gruesomely wired shut and left to suffer amidst the cold and the stale air of an Amish barn.

I tossed and turned throughout the night, always reaching for Thorp. Somehow, touching him and snuggling him assured me that the others waiting for rescue would be OK.

I had taken his progress for granted because I still had little understanding of what his life before had been like. One day, he was sitting in a cage like he had done all his life. He had grown used to the lack of kindness, used to the filth and the neglect. And then, all of a sudden, he found himself on a couch, sitting next to someone petting him and loving him. It had to be a lot to take in, to understand.

Sometimes, he would come to sit on my lap and dig his front legs into me, like he was holding on. It was as though he wanted the affection, but was unsure of how to give it back.

To take companionship and the pack mentality *out* of a dog's inherent traits is to identify the very sin of the mills. It had been painful for me to watch a dog look back with a blank stare. To attempt to touch it and have it wince or shake. To see a dog who couldn't bear to acknowledge humans. It was heartbreaking, and remembering the auction still haunted me.

CHAPTER 20

GOING PUBLIC

It was one month since the auction, since Thorp came to live with us. It was amazing what could happen in a month. I was a changed human being. I had changed physically and emotionally—even spiritually.

I was indebted to hundreds of people who fought the battles of puppy mills and worldwide cruelty. Hundreds of people who, against all odds, were not giving up. I was trying to be one of those people.

While Thorp was learning about a world full of comfort and love, I was learning about a world full of pain and betrayal.

Nearly every day since the auction, I had embarked on a new part of my journey. I had written stories, contacted vets, spoke with legislators and state officials; I had written to local papers, trying to persuade them to write about puppy mills, and I had told Thorp's story to anyone who would listen.

The story of Thorp continued to spread. The publisher of *Fetch Magazine*, Joe Kojis, wanted to feature my story in three segments. I was elated. It was an honor to see Thorp's story touch the lives of others. Readers responded with shock and gratitude. Some knew of the horror, but were thrilled to see someone write about it. I gave presentations at animal control to Brownie troops and school groups. Thorp would walk around the room, greeting the children. By the end, even without my giving the graphic details of puppy mills, children would declare, "I will adopt my next dog."

It was gratifying to know that in some small way, one person at a time, I was educating the public on puppy mills. I was sharing my experience and the story of Thorp's survival and the silent truths of thousands of dogs in our country. And most important, people were listening and looking to hear more. It made the difficult, often painful journey more bearable.

CHAPTER 21

I.D.

Thorp and I were lying on the couch when I looked up at him. I noticed his ID tag with his name and our address and phone number etched on it. It was dangling on his collar. It had been there for a few weeks, but when I looked at it, I thought about it for the first time. #171 had a name, and an address and a family who would want to know if he got lost.

Thousands of dogs, maybe only miles from suburban homes, were known only by a number. These dogs would never know the comfort of a warm bed or the touch of a gentle hand. They would never see a ray of sunshine or feel the velvety softness of green grass beneath their paws. And they would certainly never wear an identification tag that proudly showed they were part of a family.

It was realizations like this that made me question humanity. All of these dogs, and none of them had identities. Man's best friend: nameless. It was a heartless reality.

Bill came home just as I was getting up from the couch. Before he could say anything, I burst out, "Do you realize thousands of mill dogs will die known only as a number? They will never have a name."

Thrown off guard, he said, "That *is* sad, honey." He walked upstairs to change clothes.

Abby came from around the corner. "Mom, maybe we can name them, so they won't die as only a number?"

It was her innocence that touched me. I regretted saying it so harshly, and while I knew statements like this were probably difficult for a young girl to hear, I couldn't help but believe the truth was the only thing that would change the future.

"Nut, that's sweet. I'm sure the dogs would like that. Maybe you can start a list of names?"

It was hard for me to find common ground with my family. They believed in me and supported my cause, but sadly, they just couldn't relate to my pain or understand my intense passion.

It was as if my own identity was changing. Thorp was finding his place in the world and I was, too.

CHAPTER 22

CLARITY

Every night I woke, only to see Thorp curled up next to me. I always reached for him, and then I always felt an ache in my stomach. I wondered if he ever thought about any of the other dogs he had left behind, maybe ones he had stared at day after day. Or maybe even one or two with whom he had shared a cage?

Each and every time I thought about what it must have been like for him, I teared up. Six weeks had passed, and I still couldn't forget what I had seen at the auction or how it had made me feel.

That day, Abby gave a presentation on Cesar Millan, also known as the "Dog Whisperer." He had a show on the National Geographic channel about training dogs. I got to bring Thorp in as part of the presentation and ended up talking to third graders about where he had come from. I did my best not to go over the top. I had to take my audience into consideration. But I told them about the cages and the conditions the dogs were forced to live in.

They asked great questions. The best one was, "Why don't those people treat them like pets?" In the end, all of the kids said, "Those people are mean."

Even at nine years old, with only a small amount of information, they got it. I didn't show them gross pictures. I didn't scare them. I simply said that Thorp had spent the first years of his life in a chicken-wire cage, making more puppies. That alone was enough for the nine-year-olds to say, "It sounds horrible, and the police should do something about it."

I came back from school and looked around our home. It wasn't huge, it wasn't full of expensive things, but it was full. Knickknacks graced the shelves; clothes filled my closet. We didn't need anything. Yet it seemed there was always one more thing to buy, to add to the house to "make life better." We lived a very comfortable existence. I began to realize it was also a very secluded one.

While there was a dark emptiness inside of me, I found a clarity I could never before have described or understood. Suddenly, I could see, feel and touch what I was passionate about—everything became clear. All of the clutter and the things I once held so tightly were no longer important. In fact, they were only getting in my way. I needed to clear them out so more of my energy and time could be spent on what did make me happy: changing animals' lives.

Puppy-mill dogs came from nothing—absolutely nothing. Food and water were treasures to them. Basic necessities were all they had to look forward to each day, if they did get them. Often I gazed at Thorp, snuggled up on the big easy chair. He might have curled his way into the afghan or just have been sprawled out on his back, snoring. I wondered at his glory. I, too, was learning to take a deep breath and appreciate the simple things.

All dogs could teach what is important in life: a good walk, a long nap, a delicious meal, and the importance of unconditional love. However, the plight of mill dogs reaches deeper and teaches gratitude and graciousness.

The more I learned from Thorp, the more I researched the horridness of the mills, the less I needed anything but necessities in my own life.

Everyone has a passion. I had found mine the fateful day in March at the Horst Auction when I saved Thorp. Some people search their whole lives for theirs. I was grateful I could stop filling my emptiness with nothingness and just start pursuing what mattered to me.

I had known for many years that I loved animals more than the average person did. I had placed them above many people. I had felt that deep ache in my heart whenever I heard of animal cruelty. I never knew how to channel my strong attachments, my overwhelming emotions. I certainly never thought a Chinese crested powder puff would teach me how.

After all of the struggle and the enlightenment, I was tempted to throw away all the material things, sell the house and go out on my mission. Truly, nothing meant as much to me at that moment in my life than changing the plight of the helpless animals.

But what makes this story real was that I couldn't just let it all go. I had a beautiful daughter and a wonderful husband, who both had lives of their own. I could never have up and left them—even for my most important cause, animal welfare.

And that made it all the more complex and emotional. If I had been twentysomething, I could have taken off and taken on all of it. At thirty-seven, that was not really an option. So, I spent my days telling people about the mills, writing letters to legislators, volunteering at my local shelter and working with Best Friends, sharing my story and hoping it would change others like it had changed me.

I walked through my neighborhood the next morning. I needed to get a grasp on my life. There was so much going on. I felt overwhelmed by all of it.

I loved my writing position at Best Friends, but I needed to find time to get everything done. There was always too much to do. So, I walked and thought about getting fit and eating better, and I found myself mesmerized by the homes in my picket-fence subdivision.

I thought about how easy it would be to live in suburbia and never be concerned or affected by something as tragic as puppy mills. Among the tulips and the pruned hedges, and the perceived lack of cruelty, it was hard to fathom such an atrocity in this country.

Sometimes, I wished I didn't know about them. I wished that I had never seen the auction with my own eyes so that I didn't have to feel so guilty and so responsible.

But, one simple walk, and I realized I was actually blessed. Blessed to not be sheltered by the false beauty of the yards and the nice homes. I was not a prisoner in my home, locked up and unaware of what was going on in the rest of the world.

Like a hermit crab who ducks in his shell when he senses danger, my neighbors and friends tended to guard themselves against all that hurt and was unfair. Sometimes, I wished I had that shell, that safe place to hide. However, I was grateful to have faced my fears and to be doing something about them.

I was also grateful for the opportunity to follow my passion. We were fortunate enough that I could stay home and be with Abby. I enjoyed my time with her and being able to volunteer at the school. But for me, that wasn't enough. I needed to do more. I needed to offer a part of myself on behalf of what mattered to me. Some parents stay home and make their children and their households their full-time jobs. That wasn't for me.

Maybe to some it is selfish, but I needed more. I'd always had a yearning to save animals, to rescue and protect them. Not having to be gainfully employed meant I could use some of my time and talent to follow that yearning and give back. That is who I am and will always be.

People often asked me and many other rescue people, "How do you do it? How do you face such horridness? How do you deal with the euthanasia and the cruelty?"

The only answer I had was, "How do we not do it?"

It wasn't that I didn't cry or didn't have nightmares. I had endless sleepless nights, tossing and turning and questioning the state of society when animal cruelty and neglect ran rampant. People like me didn't do it because we could handle it or because it was easy for us; we did it because others wouldn't. And because deep in our hearts was a place that none of us could accurately describe, though we knew it well. It was a place in our hearts that had drawn us towards animals all of our lives. Somehow, we related to them. Somehow, more than anything else, we fought for them to be safe, to be free, to be loved.

We never really had a choice but to do it.

CHAPTER 23

OTHERS LIKE ME

With all that was going on around me, it made sense to accept an invitation to the Illinois Animal Welfare Federation Conference. It felt unbelievable to be surrounded by people like me. Everyone at the conference was there to seek out knowledge that would help them further their work and ultimately end the cycle of homeless pets.

There were workshops and lectures: shelter cleanliness, reading and understanding dog temperament, humane education and many more topics. One of the workshops I chose to attend was Compassion Fatigue.

Months earlier, I had left animal control because I was burned out. I was emotionally spent, and I had nothing left to give. I guess, in many ways, I was a lot like the dogs at the auction. I had checked out because I was so overwhelmed and under rewarded.

I knew I suffered from compassion fatigue. I hated letting go, but I knew I had no other option than to walk away from it—for a while. During that "break," I found my Best Friends writing opportunity, and we also began the work of founding a charity in conjunction with animal control.

While I was still involved with animal welfare, I had removed myself from being hands-on with the animals at the shelter. My heart had built a wall to keep me safe from the direct hurt.

However, no wall was high enough to protect me the day of the auction. Instead, I had found myself in my most vulnerable state—in my most dreaded nightmare. It wasn't just one dog or cat that needed a home and would never get one; it was hundreds of them.

I couldn't help but ponder not only why I was there, but also why the world was so full of cruelty. It seemed that no matter where I looked, some form of malice was taking place. Between the mistreatment of farm animals, canned hunting (where exotic animals are contained on private property so hunters can shoot and take home a trophy kill), and faux fur which turned out to be that of domestic dogs, my stomach ached and my heart bled.

I was flooded with guilt because I knew deep down I couldn't fix it all. I couldn't even make a dent in the puppy-mill callousness; how on earth would I change the world for animals?

Most of my close friends were not animal-welfare advocates. They had dogs and cats and other pets and treated them well, but they weren't attending protests or volunteering at shelters. I couldn't describe to them the guilt I felt. To them, the world sucked sometimes, but they each found a way to sleep soundly at night.

So, I had high expectations for the Compassion Fatigue workshop. As I walked into the room, I immediately noticed that it was packed. There wasn't an empty seat in the house. Obviously, among other animal people, I was not alone.

In her first few sentences, the speaker, author Linda R. Harper, pulled me right in. She talked about how each of us probably had a similar story about how we had been saving animals since we were young children. She explained how she used to save the stuffed animals at the Salvation Army. She and her sister would rescue all the unwanted stuffed toys and bring them home so they could be loved.

"I did that," I thought to myself. The older and more ragged they became, the more my love and compassion for them grew.

She went on to ask, "How many of you feel guilty for the way the world is? How many of you focus on the bad and, no matter the situation, assume the worst about people?"

I could feel a strange sense of relief come over me. That was exactly how I was feeling. Whenever I drove by a pasture, I assumed the horses were starving. Whenever I drove by the Amish up north, I assumed they were running a puppy mill.

I had made myself sick eating a piece of chicken and simultaneously picturing the way it had sat crowded in a factory and was later slaughtered. I couldn't even look at a burger without picturing the footage the HSUS had taken of the downed cow tortured in a California slaughterhouse earlier in the year.

It was suffocating to feel the crushing sense of cruelty encircling the world I lived in. I found I was unable to eat, to sleep and to live joyfully anymore.

She went on to explain that we will never survive in this field if we can't find a way to let go of some of the horror and to make peace with each step of progress we make, no matter how small it appears.

"There are too many animals in need and not enough rescuers to save them all," she said. "And that means you have to have ways to cope. You have to force yourself to accept you cannot do it all. You have to say no even when it feels awful. You have to find other joy in your life."

She handed out this poem. I had only seen the last passage on a website before. She had people in the class take turns reading each line. I was sitting in the back, tears streaming down my cheeks. The poem was beautiful. It represented everything I felt and believed in, and I felt like I finally understood my place in the world.

I am an Animal Rescuer
by Annette King

My job is to assist God's creatures
I was born with the need to fulfill their needs
I take in new family members without plan, thought or selection
I have bought dog food with my last dime
I have patted a mangy head with a bare hand
I have hugged someone vicious and afraid
I have fallen in love a thousand times
And I have cried into the fur of a lifeless body

I have Animal Friends and friends who have animal friends
I don't often use the word "pet"
I notice those lost at the roadside
And my heart aches
I will hand raise a field mouse
And make friends with a vulture
I know of no creature unworthy of my time

I want to live forever if there aren't any animals in Heaven
But I believe there are
Why would God make something so perfect and leave it behind
We may be master of the animals
But the animals have mastered themselves
Something people still haven't learned

War and Abuse makes me hurt for the world
But a rescue that makes the news gives me hope for mankind
We are a quiet but determined army
And making a difference every day

There is nothing more necessary than warming an orphan
Nothing more rewarding than saving a life
No higher recognition than watching them thrive

There is no greater joy than seeing a baby play
Who only days ago was too weak to eat

I am an Animal Rescuer
My work is never done
My home is never quiet
My wallet always empty
But my heart is always full

(Reprinted with permission from Annette King, Wildheartranch.org)

The entire conference was inspiring to me. I was quietly seeking my purpose within the field. I pondered at each session . . . Hmmm, humane education? That sounded like a great way to impact the future. I could go into the schools in Woodstock and talk to the students at all levels . . . Animal behavior? That seemed increasingly interesting. I could do research and learn all the intricacies of the shelter animals and be able to consult on how to place them in homes.

Throughout the conference, I found myself starving to get back into the trenches. I missed the animal work. Working at animal control was challenging because while they did their best, it would never be the shelter I envisioned dedicating my life to. There were too many politics in a government-run facility. I questioned myself and began thinking that perhaps it was time to seek out the shelter I did envision and look into real employment.

When I would come home at night, I wanted to talk incessantly about all the intriguing facts I had learned, but my dear husband didn't share my level of interest. While he appreciated my enthusiasm, he didn't need to know that cats do not partake in a social hierarchy. He didn't want to learn the sociability cues to look for in a puppy. He didn't understand why a ten-day holding period could easily lead to much more shelter overcrowding than a five-day period. He was puzzled by my excitement when I told him I had talked to PetSmart Charities about PetSmart Inc.'s recent decision to ban bully breeds from their daycare and training classes.

I had spent the day surrounded by people just like me, only to come home and find myself alone again in my journey.

I never resented Bill or any of my friends for not understanding my passion. In some ways, I think animal people don't expect to be understood. Perhaps we just accept that we are different and that our hearts ache for animals in a way that is different from all others. I could live with not being understood. I couldn't live with animal cruelty.

Sometimes it got overwhelming, thinking about all the animals suffering in the world. Should I be a vegetarian? What companies should I protest because they tested products on animals? Couldn't go to the circus; they beat the elephants. No more shopping at PetSmart because they chose to ban pit bulls and other "bully" dog breeds from their hotels and training classes. I could no longer watch horse races because of the wrongful death of Eight Belles at the Kentucky Derby.

I went to bed at night with my head spinning and my heart hurting. Why was the world so cruel and harsh? Why were there so many people who didn't seem to respect nature and its creatures? How much longer before they got it? How many more PETA protests? How many more anti-cruelty laws?

It became increasingly difficult to understand why people didn't acknowledge or act on animal cruelty. I broke them into two categories. One was made up of people who see themselves as higher on the food chain. They find comfort in the hierarchy: humans on top, animals beneath. In the second were people who didn't want to know about cruelty because they couldn't cope with atrocities. I was trying to accept that it wasn't that they didn't care about the animals; it was that they weren't wired to be strong enough to cope with such horror.

Sometimes, I just wanted to curl into a ball and hide. I wanted to pretend I didn't know about any of it. I wanted to be one of the ignorant people who were just aghast when they heard about puppy mills or farm-animal cruelty. I wanted to be oblivious.

But then, I would read one of those rescue poems or meet with a fellow animal activist, and my faith was renewed. I realized that I was given this passion for animals as a gift. The pain and the agony was to be endured, with the hope and belief that I, as just one person, could slowly begin to make a difference. I had to try.

CHAPTER 24

THE TURTLE

The dogs and I went to the cabin to get away and breathe. I was working on a story and watched as Thorp's chest rose and fell with each sigh. He was snuggled against the arm of the sofa, basking in the warmth of the sun and the cool lake breezes billowing in. Looking at him brought me a moment of peace.

More than anything, I loved that he was happy.

The last couple of months had been quite a struggle for me. The realization of so much wrong in animal welfare turned my soul upside down. It seemed like there would never be enough of anything to make everything better.

But a drive from town brought me a sign that I was not alone in the fight.

I was coming home from town when I saw a painted turtle making its way across the street. As I drove by him, I could see he was hiding in his shell. For a million reasons, I kept going even though my gut told me to stop and help him cross.

I told myself I needed to let go of being responsible for every little thing. I needed to give myself a break. I kept driving to the cabin, all the while second-guessing my decision not to help the turtle.

In about a mile, I was home and letting the dogs out. They were happy to see me, but the whole time they were out, I was thinking about the damn turtle. I couldn't take it anymore. I got the dogs back in the house and left to save the turtle.

I was worried that he might have already met with disaster, and then I would really be upset with myself. I drove and drove until I was back in town. I never saw the turtle, not even smashed on the road.

I turned around to go home and retraced my tracks, but still no turtle. The only answer was that someone else had helped him across, or maybe he had done it himself.

More than likely, with the traffic and the distance he had to go, someone helped him. That meant the world to me. I had been wrongly assuming that everyone else was out to hurt animals; I had never considered that another driver would save him.

I had no doubt that I would stop and rescue the next turtle I saw, but it was more than reassuring to find I was not alone. There were other people out there looking out for animals.

It was important to know this because there were so many days when I felt alone and overwhelmed that I wanted to give up. Small signs like the turtle gave me the strength and the courage to keep going.

CHAPTER 25

HERITAGE

The next auction was getting close, and I found myself still angered by the lack of attention from the AKC, so I wrote them a letter instead of relying on e-mails:

AKC Investigations and Inspections
8051 Arco Corp. Drive
Suite 100
Raleigh, NC 27617-3390

August 19, 2008

To Whom It May Concern:

On March 12, 2008 I rescued/purchased an AKC-registered Chinese crested powder puff from an Amish puppy mill auction in Thorp, WI held at Horst Stables.

This dog was in horrendous shape. His fur was so badly matted that it had to be shaved to his skin. I am enclosing a document from my vet office detailing his many medical conditions. I fully realize that the AKC does not guarantee health, but my concern is that you are allowing these AKC animals to be bred in a world of filth and cruelty.

The breeder who sold my dog at the auction is Melvin Kuhns Jr. (I also listed his address and license number.)

The breeders where the Chinese crested was born are Lara Dane and Kiley Stark (They applied for a registered name as "Hairless Hounds" in August of 2002) and the owner is Heather Myers of Hancock, WI.

The dog I rescued was named DJ IV on his certificate and his AKC number is TR53712702. He is a male born on 8-3-03.

I am also adding the name of the vet who supposedly vaccinated the dog two weeks prior to the auction because I feel he has failed to act in the best interest of the animal. This dog should have been taken from the owner immediately. His name is Dr. Steven Hines. (I also listed his address and license number)

I am attending another auction on September 24 and will be looking specifically for more dogs from these breeders. I do hope that the AKC can find the time and resources to investigate the dozens of hellacious mills operating in central WI. It is nothing short of inhumanity, what is going on. And until the AKC sets standards and holds breeders accountable for their operations, the cruelty these dogs endure should be on your conscience.

Rebecca Monroe

The AKC was an organization people had faith in. People relied on the AKC and the papers they handed out to mean something. People believed their dogs were worth more because they were registered with the AKC. They believed their dogs came from good breeding stock. The truth was the AKC had no idea where the dogs physically came from. All the AKC knew was that they received a minimal registration fee and some documents detailing who the sire was and who the bitch was.

I found out in the book *Saving Gracie* by Carol Bradley that when the Amish began breeding dogs, the AKC paperwork was cumbersome, and they were unable to fill it out completely. So, the AKC sent out representatives to help the Amish understand the necessary documentation. The Amish found that breeding dogs was an easy business for them. They could make a lot of money while investing little to nothing in the dogs. They didn't even need electricity.

In a strange turn of events, I got in touch with the breeders who owned Thorp's parents. After spending hours staring at the AKC papers and questioning their worth, I decided to search the Internet for their names. And in a few seconds, they were in front of me on the screen. I e-mailed the two of them together. One had the male and the other the female: Thorp's mom and dad. This was the e-mail I sent:

> I am withholding judgment until I hear from you – but I rescued one of your powder puffs from an Amish puppy-mill auction in Thorp, WI. He was so badly matted and ill that he was unrecognizable. I am curious as to how such a responsible breeder would allow this to happen and am anxious to hear what you have to say . . .

His AKC name is DJ IV and his AKC reg. number is TR53712702. He was born August 3, 2003.

The first reply came from the sire's owner:

Hi,

Thank you for rescuing this little guy. I looked him up on AKC, and he was a puppy that was out of a bitch that was owned by a gal in Michigan that bred her to my male. I was not involved in the placement of any of the puppies. But I have forwarded this e-mail on to her to see if she can give me any input on where he was sold to originally.

I try to be very careful on where my puppies go. I know the gal that owns the bitch would not have knowingly sold the puppy to a puppy mill. Her dogs are housedogs and she tries to be very careful where they are placed. Sometimes, though, people can mislead you about their intentions. The people that purchased the dog originally may have sold him to someone else.

Thank you for letting me know about this.

Lara Dane

I replied:

Dear Lara,
I appreciate that you responded so quickly to my e-mail. Thorp as I call him is "famous." His story has been published in a WI magazine and is currently on the web at Fetchmag.com and bestfriends.org. I have contacted the AKC about him. I also just posted his recent information on a Chinese crested site: http://www.chinesecrested.no/en/registry/74448/Moe+Joe+11.html#dogGalImgForm
I never realized how easy it would be to track down his heritage. He is the first so-called purebred I have owned.
It seemed to me that you and Kiley Stark (who I also e-mailed) formed the Hairless Hounds organization in 2002. Is she who placed the puppies?

I apologize if you are a decent breeder, but I have seen puppy mills firsthand and have absolutely ZERO tolerance for anyone involved in them. Even though I have been involved in animal welfare for years, when I rescued Thorp, my life changed and my mission became to end puppy mills.

Do you know how I could locate his offspring?

Thanks,
Becky

Another reply:

Hi Becky,

I have been raising and showing Chinese crested since 1993, and Kiley started getting interested in the breed when we met in 1997. She got two bitches from me and I helped her along the way. We have learned so much about the breed since I started and have really stressed breeding the best quality dogs that we can. Kiley is so upset about this she is going home tonight to find out exactly who she had sold him to originally. Then contact them to find out how he ended up where you found him.

We try and screen people very carefully, and back then Kiley doesn't think that she sold any puppies in the litter on full AKC registration. But she wants to double-check. Can you tell me what color the border is around his AKC papers? That can tell me a lot. They are either white with a purple border or white with an orange border.

As far as locating his offspring it would depend on if whoever used him for breeding registered the puppies. If so you should be able to find out something on the AKC database. I think there is a link to see the progeny of a specific dog. There is a fee for the report but I think it is minimal.

Again I want to thank you very much for contacting me about him. It sounds like you have made him a wonderful home, which is exactly what he deserves. As do all dogs. I feel the same way about puppy mills as you do. I have heard about the dog auctions but have never been to one because I know it would just break my heart to see the conditions of the dogs. I would want to take all of them. I have 10 cresteds and all of them are our housedogs. We do not have a kennel. Ours are part of our family. They sleep up in our bedroom and spend their evenings lying on the couch watching TV with us.

Please feel free to contact me or Kiley if you ever have any questions about Thorp. We are always available.

Thank you again so much for saving him.

Sincerely,
Lara Dane

I finally heard from the other breeder:

Hello Becky,

First off I would like to thank you for rescuing him. I am very upset to hear that one of our pups has had to live in such a place. How is he?

We are very careful in choosing homes that we feel will be loving, lifelong homes for them. I am very upset that someone that I trusted to be that for him has put him in such a situation. When we place puppies in homes we let the new owner know if there is any situation that arises that will uproot our puppy to contact us. So, I can assure you that I have known nothing about this or we would have stepped in to take him. I will be looking him up tonight to try to figure out how this has happened.

Please know that I take this very seriously. Our cresteds are part of our family. They are not kennel dogs. They live very full, happy lives. Socialization is very important to us. It makes me so sad to think that after raising them, and socializing them with any and all situations that will help them lead full, happy lives, that this can still happen. We consider screening the potential owners as just the next important step in raising happy, healthy, well-adjusted puppies. We try so hard to keep this very thing from happening.

I am very disturbed that this has happened.

Is there any other information that you may have that will help me to figure this out? I have contacted AKC and learned the name of the person that I originally sold him to. Her name was Heather Myers, which I will be confirming tonight when I research it.

I originally became involved in Chinese cresteds through an amazing lady named Lara of Hairless Hounds. We are very much alike in that we are both total animal lovers. When I met her she had been showing Chinese cresteds for a few years. Since then she has learned (and taught me) so much about Chinese cresteds. When you start out working with a breed because you love them, there is really nowhere to go but better. She is a very responsible breeder and has taught me to be the same. I am saddened because this has put her in the middle of this, and I have in no way meant to hurt this puppy or Lara's reputation. This was a puppy that I am responsible for, not Lara.

Above all, I am so happy that Thorp has found what I was originally hoping for him. A loving, lifelong home. Thank you for taking him out of such a miserable place and giving him so much to look forward to. Though I am sad that it took him this long to find it, I appreciate what you have done for him. As corny as this sounds: please give him a hug for me.

I will be researching this tonight. Please feel free to contact me at any time. Thank you again for what you have done. I look forward to hearing from you.

Sincerely,
Kiley Stark

My reply:

Kiley,

I am somewhat relieved to hear that his original home was a safe and loving one. I get so sad when I look at him and think about his past. He was in such bad shape when I got him.

He was the worst one at the auction and the oldest (5 yrs.) - and that is why I picked him.

I bought him from an Amish man named Melvin Kuhns. I never met this man but that is what the paperwork says. To give you an indication of how pathetic this all is, I bought him for around $60. It still makes me cry.

The owner on the AKC papers is Heather Myers, and her address on the paper is Hancock, WI (which is near Pardeeville).

While I have always been involved in animal welfare, my life changed drastically after attending that auction. I have made a commitment to educating people on the horrors of puppy mills as well as the AKC's lack of support in ending the mills. As a breeder, I realize you might support that organization, but I believe they deserve the cruelty these dogs endure to hang on their shoulders. If they would stop issuing certificates to anyone who applies, uneducated people would stop buying these so-called purebreds from pet stores and on the Internet.

Thorp is the first purebred I have ever owned. All of my other dogs are mutts from shelters. But when I attended that auction and saw him – I knew I had to get him out of there.

He has adjusted fairly well. When I first got him, he shook constantly. Anything new scared him so much. His teeth are in really bad shape. He is very attached to me. He gets along great with our two other dogs and three cats. He has learned to walk on a leash, to go for car rides and is still learning to potty outside. New places and new things still scare him, but he doesn't shake nearly as much.

I wouldn't trade him for the world. We share a very special bond and I believe we changed each other's lives – both for the good.

If you are interested, you can read his story on www.fetchmag.com or at www.bestfriends.org. His rescue has become famous. So much so, that I am in the process of making a book out of it.

I had no idea it would be this easy to trace his lineage or I would have done it months ago. Though for the first few months after the auction, I was having a hard time just coping with what I saw. I spent a lot of my time contacting WI legislators and the vet who vaccinated him prior to the auction and the head humane officer/vet for the state of WI. I have been in shock at how few laws there are in WI regulating this "industry." And sadly, how few people care in central WI about the rampant puppy mills.

The last 6 months have been quite a whirlwind to me.

I appreciate your time and hope that perhaps, our relationship can help us both find the peace and justice we are looking for. What happened to Thorp should never happen to any dog.

Thank you,

Her reply:

Hi Becky,

I read your article and found myself in tears. What a horrible thing. I'm sure it is just beyond comprehension. It is disturbing to think there are so many puppy mills and so close, too. When you think of these, I always think of Southern states. I live in MI so this is very close to home. It makes me sick to think that Thorp was a part of that. I want to thank you for being brave enough to walk into that place and do what you did and have been doing. I just can't begin to imagine what that must have been like.

I researched last night and found that the person that I originally placed Thorp with was a Debbie Jones in Pardeeville, WI. She either misrepresented herself and snowed me on the type of person she is, or she placed him after the fact, not knowing whom she was really placing him with.

Although we work within the AKC standards, etc., we totally agree that there should be more representation and follow-through with breeders such as these. I do not know how they can stand back and watch this without changing things to make it impossible to continue. My understanding is that any breeder registering 7 or more litters a year can be and are inspected. How can places like this stay under the radar? You would think that somewhere along the way, AKC would have to know about this . . . ???

We are small, responsible breeders. We take the health and happiness of our cresteds very seriously as well as breed for genetically sound, healthy puppies. We have patellas checked and eyes certified. We also have begun working with a new form of DNA testing that checks for genetic markers for dozens of both inherent and genetic diseases. We are under the belief that if you can't do this properly and won't do what's right for these animals, then don't do it at all.

Quite a few years ago, Lara had helped to rescue a group of dogs that we placed among friends and family. These were all cresteds that had been in horrendous conditions in a puppy mill down South. I think that my mom's is the last of them after close to 10 years, I would guess it's been. Some of them recovered and adapted quickly, and others it took a long time learning to cope with things.

Mom's Maggie was probably one of the worst cases that we took part in rescuing. I can happily say that she is a happy, content part of the family now. It's so frustrating that one of the main things that we love about companion animals is that from day one, they instinctually have a love of life, and then people break that spirit. It takes quite a bit of love and care to help them learn to love life again. I am so happy that Thorp has you to help him through this.

Thank you for the pictures of him. I was heartbroken to hear about this and see how he looked, but am very happy to know he has you. I truly enjoyed seeing him in the 2nd picture. I can tell he is in a very happy place in his life.

When is the fall auction that you spoke about? If there is anything we can do to help out, please let us know. Also, if you ever make it this way, please let me know. We can get together and you can meet my furry kids!

Just a little side note: When Thorp was a puppy my nickname that I had for him was "Trouble," which is how I have him identified in my records alongside his AKC number. I loved seeing his picture, sprawled in a comfy position in the grass. It goes to show what a little love and compassion can do for these innocent creatures.

Again, please let me know if there is anything we can do to help.

Sincerely,
Kiley

My reply:

Dear Kiley,

Thank you for reading my story – I think it's important for everyone to read so that there is a better understanding of the actual horrors of these mills. I especially have a "thing" for the Amish because everyone thinks they are such kind and gentle people . . .

I am curious – on my AKC paper for him, it says that Heather Myers was the owner? I have often thought about contacting her . . . should it really be this Debbie? I know I can't change the past, but I also think it's important that people know what their actions led to.

May I ask if there was an agreement about getting Thorp neutered? I always thought that if a "family" adopts a purebred, there is a contract that states the dog must be spayed/neutered so that there isn't any accidental breeding which could affect the lineage of the breed?

It's actually an interesting twist to the whole story . . . he was born in a good home and yet still found a way to a miller's hands. It makes it all scarier – how many dogs were leading good lives and then found themselves like this?

I won't know until a week before the next auction what types of dogs will be sold. When I rescued Thorp, the Chinese Crested Rescue had offered to take him, but I just couldn't let him go. They were great. They gave me a lot of background on the breed and were always there for questions. But if there happen to be any CCs at the auction, would you be interested in helping save them?

I will keep in touch. I really am writing a book with the hope someone will publish it, so I might have future questions, and having you as a reference could be really helpful – if you don't mind.

By chance, maybe you could help with this . . . I have the miller's name and dealer's license – do you have a way of searching that in the AKC system? Or maybe that is just with the WI of AG?

Kiley, I appreciate your concern and sincerity and sharing what you remember about "Trouble!" These days, Trouble is just a very sweet, needy little guy who wants nothing more than to be safe and loved.

I hope we can stay in touch.

Our last conversation:

Hi Becky,

Debbie purchased a show prospect and assured us that she had every intention of showing him. Thorp was placed with her because the 1st puppy that she had gotten only had 1 testicle and 2 are required for showing in the AKC rings (at 12 weeks it can sometimes be hard to tell this, a lot of times they do not "drop" until later). So since she had purchased a show prospect, we then placed the original puppy in a wonderful pet home in Louisiana, and Thorpe went to live with Debbie. It is so hard to hear that someone that we believed could have deceived us like this. I guess when we always do what we say we are going to do, it's hard to disbelieve others. I am hoping that Thorp wasn't intentionally placed but was placed with someone that she thought would be a good home for him. I would like to believe this because after thinking about it, the first puppy would physically be able to breed with only 1 testicle, and the whole thing was revolving around the fact that she couldn't show him. I wouldn't think that a miller or someone that is just breeding for money as the Amish must do would care about this trait. They are not in it to improve the breed as we try to do, or breed genetically sound puppies, like we do.

We do contracts with each puppy that leaves. In that contract we have a spay/neuter agreement for what AKC calls limited registration. We do not send papers

165

until we have a letter from a veterinarian on their letterhead stating that the puppy was spayed or neutered. And then we will send them their papers, but at that time, they are still only receiving limited registration papers.

In regards to rescue, we have talked it over and come up with a way that we can help. Since we aren't in a position to bring these poor dogs into our homes, we would like to offer a page on our website to devote to rescues. We have a lot of people that contact us, looking to give a dog a great home. We would be able to post pictures and info and an e-mail address that they could contact for more information.

www.akc.org/classified/search/ind ex.cfm is a page that may help you with tracking the miller if they are an AKC breeder. I tried tracking any breeder in WI, and also for cresteds, and it came back with nothing.

Anyway, I hope we have in some way helped.

Please let us know if you are
interested in the rescue page.

Sincerely,
Kiley

It was an interesting twist I didn't see coming. Thorp started with what appeared to be real breeders, not a puppy mill. I wanted to believe they were one of the good ones. But it was hard for me to believe any breeders were good. Yet everything Lara and Kiley described indicated that they were ideal breeders. They researched the people who wanted to buy the dogs. They wouldn't place them with just anybody. They had a contract stating whether the dog could be bred in the future. They stated that if circumstances changed, they would take the dog back. And, even though I didn't see their homes, they both emphasized how the dogs lived with them.

The puppies in pet stores weren't sold under any of these circumstances. No one cares who buys a puppy at a pet store. The pet store never offers to take the dog back. The store doesn't care if the dog gets bred in the future. And that is why the assumption that good breeders would never sell their puppies in stores is accurate. Good breeders are invested in the puppies and their reputations, not the dollars they bring in.

I decided I wouldn't take the search any further. I didn't want to get involved in other people's lives. There were days I pictured walking up to their door, knocking and asking them if Thorp was their dog. There were days I pictured hitting them when they said, "Yes."

Once in awhile, I would catch myself in a total daydream, thinking Thorp ran away and ended up in the wrong hands. But, unless he carried his AKC papers in his mouth while he was running away, his transfer of ownership to a mill was intentional. I never could make sense of that.

CHAPTER 26

NEVER ENOUGH

Thorp's story was growing. If what they said was true, he was born into a home where he was allowed to play like a puppy. His life started as it should have, but then by some twist of fate, he was sold or stolen and found himself in a dark barn. His only purpose, to reproduce. I had proof of his lineage, and now I had proof of some of the pups he had sired. Thorp's life had never been his own.

It wasn't exactly what I wanted, but it was a great compromise. The breeders couldn't actually rescue any of the mill dogs, but they were willing to post adoptable dogs on their website. I excitedly contacted the Chinese Crested Rescue. Unfortunately, according to the National Chinese Crested Rescue, they were not allowed to intermingle with breeders. They wouldn't be able to place their contact info on the breeders' website.

How disappointing and sad for other Chinese cresteds needing rescues. And Chinese Crested wasn't the only rescue with this policy.

Being somewhat of an outsider, it was hard for me to make sense of the rules and regulations rescues place on themselves—which often hindered successful adoptions. One example was the regulation of fences. Many rescues require that anyone adopting any dog must have a fence. Without the fence, the person or family is unable to adopt, even a dog who is not a runner.

HSUS cited it as a bad reason to deny adoption. According to statistics, dogs in homes with fences actually get less exercise than dogs without fences. Fenceless dogs are exercised more frequently by their owners.

Other rescue rules include: how many hours the dog will be home alone, number of other animals in the home, ages of the children, yard size, etc. There are valid reasons for all of these questions. However, it is important to take into account the whole picture. A person who wants to adopt shouldn't be denied because they don't meet all of the criteria.

Worse than the rules of rescues can be their attitudes. An acquaintance told me of her family's experience trying to adopt a pit bull. They owned two small dogs and were looking to adopt a pit bull or pit mix because they had heard these dogs were unwanted, and so many were being euthanized. When they inquired at rescues and shelters, they were laughed at. It is true that not all pit bulls are good with other dogs (small or big), but from my own experience at the county shelter, I knew there are pit bulls who are great with other dogs. Surely, with all the pit bulls in need of homes, there was one whom they could have adopted. Sadly, in the end, they bought a dog from the local pet store.

The rescues, who take in dogs from mills, send potential adopters into the doors of the very places they are trying to close down, all because of their shortsightedness.

I realized that people working in rescues and shelters are tired of dealing with ignorant owners. They are tired of the excuses and neglectful behaviors. But there are good people out there who are trying to do the right thing. It is critical that rescues and shelters don't turn them away, or leave the families telling others they will never try to adopt another dog because their experience of trying to adopt was a bad one.

Rescues and shelters must be willing to work with people. They must mindfully and kindly educate and assist them with finding a dog who will be the perfect match for their family and situation. With millions of homeless dogs, certainly there will always be at least one who will fit their needs.

To change the world is to change one person at a time, and that means treating each situation individually, just like the dogs who are rescued.

The entire grouping of animal-welfare people seems under constant attack. I have found that animal-welfare people tend to be chastised by those who are critical of animal rights. Instead of listening and presenting valid arguments, they react with some comment like, "If only you cared that much about neglected children or starving babies or homeless people."

It's enraging to me for a myriad of reasons. I do care about anything and anyone who is helpless and hurting. I think it is grossly unfair to take away the validity of suffering animals by one-upping it with human suffering. I believe that every soul was put on this earth for a reason. My reason has to do with helping animals. I think it is wrong to diminish my life pursuit just because someone doesn't understand it.

What I want to say to people who react in this way is this: "No, sir, I am concerned with human welfare. I would never walk by a helpless child in need, and I know neither would you. However, I would also never walk by a helpless animal, but I fear that you would—and so I pursue this fight with the hope of getting you and people like you to take a second look at the animal."

I believe a lot can be determined about a person by the way he treats a helpless creature. Regardless of money, power or fame, the way a person treats a thing in need speaks volumes about him as a human being. Something I shared in the signature of all my e-mails:

The greatness of a nation and its moral progress can be judged by the way its animals are treated.
—Mahatma Gandhi

All of my contemplation stemmed from another disturbing conversation I had while in Marquette County, Wisconsin. It is the county where we have a cabin and where Doc Hines was a state representative.

My husband and I were at a local bar and grill, having pizza, when I heard a man at the next table talking about various police cases. He went on to talk about retiring in a few years, and about so many other government issues that I knew he was a county policeman. I had enjoyed a cocktail or two and could feel my blood pumping when I envisioned asking him about the lack of humane officers in the county. I took a deep breath, and as I caught his eye, I said, "Sir, are you a policeman? I have some questions for you."

To which he responded kiddingly, "No . . ."

I said, "Well, I'm going to ask you anyway."

He said, "I hear that a lot."

I started, "Do you know many of the puppy mills are run by the Amish in Wisconsin?"

"Ah, the Amish. If I had a dollar for every call we get from someone thinking the Amish are starving their horses. Why is it that people don't care about starving kids?"

Reluctant to let the conversation go off course, I continued, "Do you have pets?"

"Yes, and I treat them well. I take them to Dr. Hines on a regular basis."

My stomach flipped. "Ugh, *that* vet," I thought to myself.

"Dr. Hines is actually the vet who vaccinated my mill dog, yet overlooked the poor condition he was in."

I couldn't stop myself and kept rambling, "I also had a conversation with his father, who attempts to understand the puppy-mill situation while still supporting antiquated regulations like 'dog damages.' I'm frustrated with the stance Wisconsin takes on animal welfare."

I was getting so mad. How was I the only one seeing the larger picture?

"Do you know Dr. Bellay? I discussed this with her, and she said she's trying to get a humane officer trained in each of the counties."

The policeman sighed. The kind of sigh that only expresses disgust.

The man seated with him finally spoke up, "Yes, I have heard that. We need humane officers. Marquette County has been considering participating, and I think we have an officer interested."

He looked right at me and said, "I agree with you, miss. More needs to be done."

The other policeman just shook his head and went back to his meal. I turned to my husband with sad eyes.

And as he had said many times before, he repeated, "Not everyone cares about it like you do."

It was not that I expected them to. I think it was that I believed with all of my heart that if I shared what I had learned, it would make a difference. Because I knew, above all else, things had to be different.

CHAPTER 27

DARKNESS AND HOPE

I found it odd that whenever Thorp got the chance, he lay in the sun. So many other dogs find shade to rest in and be cool. I wondered if it was the years of darkness that made Thorp look for the warmth and hope of the sun. It had been nearly six months, and when I noticed things like this about him, I still wanted to cry. It was as if my tears would wash away all the pain and cruelty he had endured.

The fall auction was only two weeks away. What was once an unknown to me was glaringly real and fast approaching. I had already started to have nightmares about what I would see again.

There was talk of the September auction being even worse than the last. The economy was struggling, and that affected so much. Many of the breed rescues were saying that they couldn't rescue any dogs because of the lack of funds and minimal space and foster homes they had available. To make things more difficult, even the puppy millers were being squeezed by the failing economy and finding that they couldn't sell their dogs anymore. Which, sadly, led them to dumping the dogs, or worse . . . A month earlier, in Pennsylvania, a couple of millers had shot and killed eighty of their stock, one at a time.

My heart ached to think of the poor, helpless dogs taken out of their cages and shot one by one. The thought of those dogs hearing each of the eighty shots and the cries of the other dogs, all while they awaited their own grim fate. Perhaps, a fate better than the lives they endured, but certainly not worthy of the souls they each had.

In the same period of time, Puppy Haven, one of the largest puppy mills in the state of Wisconsin, sold its entire facility and all 1200 of its dogs to the Wisconsin Humane Society. The funds were raised from generous donors. It was the first deal of its kind in the country. Wallace Havens, the infamous designer of the mini Saint Bernard, was no longer in business. And the property was deeded to never again have any puppy-mill activities take place.

1200 dogs were free.

The auction was a week away. The last time, I'd had no idea what to expect, and while that had made me uneasy, it had also left room for the hope that things wouldn't be as bad as I envisioned. I knew better the second time around.

I questioned going to the auction. I was not representing a shelter or a rescue—I was just a person. Just one person in the middle of a problem much bigger than I could understand. But I was trying, and in my search for answers, I found myself contemplating the meaning of life in general. I was not a religious person as far as organized religion was concerned. But I believed there must be something to find peace in. Something that reinforced my own belief in doing what was right. No God or Being could approve of what I had witnessed, so how was I supposed to make sense of it?

Sometimes I felt that my compassion for animals was leading me purposely down this path, as if it was all part of the journey for me to understand the meaning of life. I never needed something bigger in my life before the auction.

I was trying to find peace with rescuing just one. I was thinking about the Serenity Prayer: having courage and patience and the wisdom to know the difference between what I could change and what I couldn't. I didn't seem to have the wisdom.

With only a few days until the auction, the list of dogs to be sold off was sent out to all who had attended the last one. It made my stomach sick. I was sad all day. I e-mailed the list to my friends and colleagues who had never been to an auction. They each called to let me know that they couldn't stop thinking about it. Most said reading the list made them want to cry.

I am not sure, psychologically, what the list did to people. There were no faces with the list—just dogs available by breed, color, sex and miller. Maybe the mere fact that the list represented furry souls to be sold like property is what scarred each of us. What we had come to love and treat nearly as equals were so blatantly bought and sold like commercial goods. It went against our beliefs, and that hurt.

There was also a lot of talk on the forum about the unscrupulous acts of the auction house. The auction house was run by Mennonites, and since more rescuers were attending, there were accusations that the millers planned to act covertly and purposely bid against rescuers. They knew we would do practically anything to get the dogs out. There were also accusations about the auction practices. There were regulations on the age and the health of the dogs to be sold at the auction. The dogs needed to be at least eight weeks old and in good health. Those issues had been in question in the past. It really was like an underground operation. And while an inspector from the United States Department of Agriculture (USDA), the same people who inspect meat, was at the auction, things appeared to be overlooked.

It was the eve of the auction. I was sitting at my cabin in central Wisconsin, contemplating how it all began.

Asking myself, "How did I get here?" In just six months, I had learned so much and had discovered a world so cruel and cold it left my heart struggling to beat again. I had been touched by such agony and torture that I couldn't bear to stomach a piece of meat. I cried in the middle of the night because I knew I couldn't save them all. And I cried in the middle of the day because I knew the world could be a different place.

There had been hundreds of e-mails among all of the rescuers attending the auction. It had been heartwarming, to say the least, to see a group of strangers work so diligently toward a common goal: saving the most dogs on auction day. Each of the people represented a different interest. Some were breed rescues, others were shelters, some were just in it to help however they could. But all were in it to change the lives of the dogs who suffered needlessly in puppy mills every day.

Six months ago, on the eve of the March auction, I was unknowing. I was scared, but I had no idea of what to expect. To walk into the auction barn blindly was a gift. I had no plan, no forethought. For the second auction, I knew exactly what I would see, and I felt nothing but helplessness.

At the first auction, Margie and I sat cringing in shock and disbelief; we were also very alone. The place was cold and dark, and we had no idea who was playing along and who was there to make a difference. We didn't know whom to trust.

Though Margie wouldn't accompany me the second time, I felt part of the group. I knew the players. I had read their hopes by e-mail, and I had shared their tears in private. For months, the group had worked towards the auction and making it more successful.

A list was formulated so that none of the rescuers would bid against each other. We submitted pictures of ourselves and identified the types of dogs we were after. When the list came out, everyone began listing which ones they would bid on and how high they would go. We were organized, and we were ready.

I had hope for the first time in a while that the entire puppy-mill issue was going to end someday. I believed that the economy would have an effect, and I even believed that the general public was becoming better educated on buying from pet stores. But most of all, I learned in the last few weeks that one critical difference between the millers and the rescuers would prevail: the rescuers had an unrelenting passion to end the horror. No business can survive against the throes of such dire passion. The rescuers saved the dogs because it was in their hearts and souls to do so. Money couldn't compete successfully against love. That was how I knew we would win the battle.

After seeing the auction list, many of my friends donated money to my cause, and I was using it towards a four-year-old goldendoodle female. I could only imagine how messed up she would be. She was the same age as Thorp had been at his auction, and she was listed by a sole miller who had no other dogs in the auction—just like Thorp.

With so many needing rescue, I looked for signs to lead me down the right path. I believed that Elmbrook Humane Society would take her and foster her and find her a home. I wanted to have a hands-on feeling that I had done something to make a difference. But my family was just settling down after Thorp had come into our lives. I struggled with what was best: to leave well enough alone or save another. I believed I would find my answer when I walked into the barn, just like last time.

I caught myself looking deeply into Thorp's eyes. He was sitting on his rug, looking out the screen door. I could see by his little nose twitching that he was taking it all in. The noises and the smells were his to enjoy. All those years locked in a cage without his freedom. A mill dog values these types of moments. It was Thorp's time to finally be a dog.

I thought about something Carol had sent me. One of the best quotes in it was, "Look back, but don't stare." Meaning, respect the dog's past, but don't make it all that he is. I loved that. It had probably taken me six months to understand it. Each time I looked at Thorp, I only saw his past. It made me sad and sick, and I think it prevented me from seeing his future or even living in his present. Thorp wasn't only a mill dog. He was a dog who enjoys life like all the other dogs do, and I needed to respect him for that.

It reminded me that when I walked back into the barn, I would see hundreds of dogs desperately wanting what Thorp had found. Tears streamed down my face because I knew what lay ahead.

Before I fell asleep on the eve of the auction, I vowed to stand tough and unwavering as I endured the dreaded day, knowing in the days that followed, all of the emotion I had held back would surface, and I would fall apart.

CHAPTER 28

AUCTION #2

It had been two weeks since my second Horst Puppy Mill Auction in Thorp, Wisconsin. It took me time to process it all.

It was very difficult to fully face what I saw or even comprehend the amazingly positive things that took place. The auction was different on so many levels—at least for me.

Going into the auction, I was part of a large group of rescuers. Some of them were breed-specific, others just willing to save whoever needed it most. We met in the parking lot an hour before the auction house opened. We met with the protesters and all talked about why we were there.

I was grateful to Chuck Wegner, executive director of the Clark County Humane Society, for making the statement, "Protestors and rescuers alike, remember that though our strategies might be very different, we all are here for the same reason: we want to end the horror of puppy mills."

I sensed that we did all respect one another—even if we didn't agree with each other. The divide between the protestors and the rescuers was a real issue that became a devastating obstacle in sending a clear message about puppy mills.

Rescuers were divided into two groups. One was willing to purchase dogs, and the other was willing to take the dogs but not pay for them. Then there were the protestors, who were willing to stand up for the cause but didn't believe in taking any of the dogs because it only provided an outlet to the breeders. There were cases to be made for all of the viewpoints. However, the day of the auction, no matter what the strategy, we were a very united group. And, in being so, I felt a strange sense of calm and courage to face the grueling hours.

For my second auction, I brought along my friend Susan and her husband, Bill. Susan had become my animal-welfare mentor. We met at animal control. We came together to start a nonprofit for the county, Friends of McHenry County Animal Control. We knew the shelter needed subsidies to provide better care for the animals. Susan had spent twenty years in animal welfare. She had managed many shelters, including the Massachusetts Society for the Prevention of Cruelty to Animals (MSPCA). Truthfully, I idolized her. She had been in the field "a long time" and was patiently teaching me so many things. After learning about my first auction and seeing how it had traumatized me, she wanted to go with me to support me and to see it for herself. With all she had done, she had never been to one. I was grateful to have her with me.

The day was unbearably frigid, with the windchill way below freezing. As we walked into the barn, I started to tell her that the dogs would be over to the right. I suddenly realized that the comfort I felt simply because of familiarity had disappeared. The dogs weren't where they were last time, and immediately, I could feel my heart beat faster.

The dogs were all in chicken-wire cages, in a barn off to the back of the auction. I guessed that it was an actual puppy-mill barn. Either the auction family no longer milled, or they were using it just for the day of the auction. All of the small chicken-wire cages were permanently affixed to the concrete. The placement of the dogs will forever be burned in my brain. The images were so devastating and profound. I could never forget them.

A long row of puppies sat to the right of where I entered. Many mixes like bichon-poo and Yorkie-poo, and even a few goldendoodle pups. The designer dogs everyone wants, thanks to the celebrities who carry them around like accessories. These pups were all very young—under twelve weeks. To the left of the entrance started the Chihuahuas, miniature pinschers, Boston terriers, a long-haired Jack Russell, beagles, cairn terriers, and a

Scottish terrier. In the back were the cocker spaniels; the oldest dog, a female goldendoodle—the one I wanted to get out; an English bulldog; and the Westies. Back up the center aisle were many cages of very scared pugs, many cages of very sick Yorkies, some toy poodles, a barely alive Shih Tzu as well as a few other Shih Tzus, some more Chihuahuas and finally, a Pekingese that they later marked a Maltese.

Certain dogs stood out. There were four Yorkies who were so ill they were barely breathing. There was a lot of talk between the rescuers and the USDA inspector of pulling them, but right before the auction, they were still there. I thought it for the best, because if they got pulled, they usually went back to the miller. What a horrible fate. So, I thought, if they were in the auction, one of us could get them out and give them the opportunity for a healthy, happy life.

Sadly, when the Yorkies came up, it was announced that they had been pulled from the auction. I still don't know what happened to them.

There was a small carrier above the Chihuahuas that had puppies so small they weren't even six weeks old. Someone tried to get them pulled, but the USDA inspector said that since the breeder was not licensed, she couldn't pull the dogs. The insanity.

The long row of frightened pugs pierced my heart. I couldn't help but think about all of the people who wanted one of those popular breeds at the pet stores and had no idea of the hell behind the glass windows. It saddened and angered me. How I wished more people would come to the auctions and see the truth.

Like in March, I silently searched for one that spoke to me. I already had funds to get the goldendoodle female out. She was in really bad shape. She was completely shut down. It didn't matter who tried to talk to her or who reached in to pet her: she didn't respond. I knew she needed to be freed.

But I couldn't help but look for another. Knowing that there were quite a few people from breed rescues, I tried to worry about the breeds that might fall through the cracks. One of those breeds was the Chihuahua. I had taken to #34, a supposed long-haired Chihuahua. He was brown and black. He wasn't badly matted, but his coat was dirty. Mostly, he was petrified of people. No matter what I did, he would not allow me to pet him or to even approach him without bolting to the other side of the cage and trembling. I marked down his number next to #55 through 58, the sick Yorkies.

While Susan, Bill and I had walked in together, we each walked to the cages on our own. The experience is a personal one. Each dog speaks to each person differently, and I believe that the pain of seeing such cruelty is so great that one needs time to endure it alone.

At the last auction, even with Margie there, I had felt incredibly alone. We didn't know who any of the people were and felt so overwhelmed by it all. This time, I knew people, and we knew each other. We had formed an online forum and had talked through it for the last six months. There was a sense of community, of teamwork, and it certainly made me feel like I could get through the day much better.

One woman, Elizabeth, whom none of us knew, showed up at the parking lot where we met. She had flown from Florida to rescue a dog because of something she had read on the Internet. We were all grateful for her presence, and each of us helped her at the auction.

When the auction started, Bill, Susan and I sat with her. She had marked down the numbers of the dogs she was interested in. We started talking, and she expressed that she was concerned about flying a possibly sick dog back to Florida. She wasn't sure how she would be able to get the dog home. Coincidentally, my parents would be driving from Wisconsin to Florida in the next few days, so I offered their services to her. I gave her one of my Best Friends business cards in case she needed to get in contact with me.

She took the card and after a few moments said, "You're Becky Monroe? You're the reason I'm here. I read your story about the last auction, and I wanted to come and rescue my own."

I had been sitting in the broken auction chair, looking around at the pitiful place; my heart breaking, wondering what I was doing there. How I was ever going to make a difference? And when I heard Elizabeth say those words, I started to cry.

A person had come thousands of miles simply because of something I wrote. A dog would be saved because of a few written words. My tears were unstoppable. It was overwhelming. It was a pivotal moment for me. It all hurt—every day—the fighting, the nightmares, the cruelty; but in one moment, it was all worth it. I was making a difference, one truthful story at a time.

What a miraculous story and such a courageous journey for Elizabeth. We endured the auction together and each contributed to a dog's new fate. Elizabeth "won" the Maltese. I could see in her eyes that no miller was going to get that dog. I know in my heart that he is now her own Thorp. I know she saw things she will never be able to explain to her friends and family who were not there, but I know she will try and tell the story to anyone who will listen. On that day, I knew that she, too, would make a difference.

I did rescue #34, for only fifty-five dollars. Like Thorp, no one wanted him but me. Unlike with Thorp, I knew what I was getting myself into, and I was just glad that I could help one more get out. I saved the goldendoodle, thanks to the generosity of caring friends back home. Before the auction, I had arranged with some of the rescuers to take her. The goldendoodle left that day for her foster home. I remember pulling her out of the cage. She stared at me with the saddest of eyes. She had given up fighting long ago. She could barely walk on a leash. She was a pale tan color, but her coat hadn't been brushed or washed in months, maybe years. Thousands of dogs are neglected every year, but seeing one, touching one, makes it so real and so horrible. To be able to free a dog from so many years of abuse is a privilege and a miracle. It is what makes the heartbreak bearable.

Susan and Bill rescued four dogs. They "donated" two basset pups to Basset Buddies and a Chihuahua puppy to Elmbrook Humane; and they kept #27, also known as "Tippy" on his tag. Bill had quickly grown fond of Tippy during the viewing hours. Tippy was very shy.

The desperately sick Shih Tzu went to Shih Tzu Rescue of Minnesota. Lin Eckland, who had become one of my closer rescuer friends, saved her. They weren't sure she would even survive the long car ride home. The little Tzu body was so frail, and she just drooped in her crate. If she were to live, it would be a miracle.

At the final count, our group of rescuers saved 50 percent of the dogs, or approximately seventy dogs. There might have been more who went to a rescue or some version of a rescue versus a miller. We only knew about those who went to our group.

The auction part ended, and we all went to pay for the lives we were so proud to save. In the meantime, a miller had approached my friend Carol about some extra Chihuahua pups he had in the car. I went to the parking lot with her, and sure enough, there were two very small pups in a crate in his car, next to two very frightened Boston terriers that his friend had bought at the auction.

She asked how much, and he said seventy-five dollars each. She explained that she had only paid forty-five dollars at the auction and couldn't afford more than twenty-five dollars each because she didn't have much money left. With those puppy eyes staring at me, I was completely taken aback by the negotiations. My heart was screaming inside, telling me, "Give her money, give her money!!"

But I knew Carol had much more experience than I did. I knew it was important to respect her position. I said nothing.

She told the Mennonite man that she would have to go back in and ask some people for money, and if she could come up with more, she would be back. He said he would wait for a while.

We walked away together, and Carol explained that I couldn't just give them what they wanted. Deep down, I knew that. Carol went and found people, asking them what they thought and what they might have to help out financially. I was watching the man's truck.

I saw him get in it to drive away and started to scream to Carol . . . But it was too late. Those two pups were gone. They were going back to the mill. My heart sank, and I thought I was going to throw up.

Carol felt terrible and said, "It wasn't meant to be." Apparently, it was not. I understood what had happened, but my heart broke into pieces, knowing what those little dogs went back to on that deathly cold day. Those two pups still haunt me.

On the good side were the numerous dogs we took out and into the rescue vans and cars. Dog after dog being brought out in loving arms with the hope of a brand-new, wonderful future. I knew we put money in those wretched people's pockets, but I didn't care. The dogs were saved from a life of misery, and that was all that mattered.

It had been almost unbearable to sit through another auction, but seeing all the rescue people come together to change the lives of helpless creatures was nothing short of miraculous. Even some of the protestors came to see who got out and were grateful for everyone's efforts.

When Elizabeth came out with her own rescue, I took her picture, right where Margie took Thorp's and mine. It was a moment of success in a small way. One by one, people were realizing the truth about puppy mills and were taking action. It wasn't as quick as I'd hoped, nor did it provide the ultimate solution I desired, but as a group, we were getting the message out and people were listening.

Each of the seventy dogs who were rescued that day had their own story to tell. Each person who would adopt them would know their story and would hopefully share it. It might be hard for some people to believe what they never see, but for every dog that gets out and tells its story, numerous people are listening and believing. Eventually, enough people will know and believe because their lives were touched in one way or another by the story of a puppy-mill dog.

CHAPTER 29

MULLY

Three weeks had passed, and as I looked at Mully (short for Mulligan, which means second chance in golf lingo) and watched him wag his tail and jump with glee, I couldn't help but reflect: Who thought puppy mills were OK? Less than a month ago, Mully, who was only known as #34, a long-haired Chihuahua, wouldn't even let me touch him through the cage. He would cower and lower his head and shake. He was so afraid of me and anyone else who would try and show him attention. He was only a year and a half old.

Mully was running and jumping and playing with toys. He snuggled up with me at night and never moved. He would stretch out his legs and roll onto his back—so trusting toward me. He would come (most of the time) when I called his name. And when I returned from an errand, he was so excited to see me. His rapid change filled my heart with joy and at the same time brought me to my knees—because there were so many more like him that needed to get out.

All of whom should never have been there in the first place.

Mully was so different from Thorp. Unlike Thorp's extremely shy behavior, Mully's reactions were quick. When Bill and Abby met him, they were surprised to see him jump and act so much more quickly than Thorp. He had energy Thorp didn't have, and yet Mully's fear of people was just as strong.

Bill and Abby were not as uneasy with Mully joining our home. They seemed to assume that an auction equaled a new dog. I had made it clear Mully was temporary. I would find him a home as soon as I felt he was ready. I was appreciative that my family had learned to cope with me and my mission, and the dogs who became a part of it.

In truth, I didn't give them a lot of options because I didn't feel like I had any. I had been presented with a life-changing moment, and continuing to act upon it was all I could do. I never questioned my actions—not once.

To my pleasant surprise, our local TV station did a two-part segment on a massive breeding facility in Minnesota owned by Kathy Bauck under the name Pick of the Litter Kennel and other aliases. She had been in business over twenty-five years and had one of the largest dog-breeding facilities in the country, selling thousands of dogs annually nationwide.

They showed footage of dogs being dumped in agricultural liquid to prevent ticks and fleas. The liquid was poison. If it got in the dogs' eyes, they could lose their sight, or if the dog licked it off their fur, they could die. They also showed undercover footage of a female bichon who couldn't deliver her last pup, so the workers at the kennel used forceps to rip it out of her. In doing so, they broke her tail and her leg and left her to die. She did die—lying on chicken wire—alone.

On top of the sadness was pure madness. The USDA didn't know if they had enough evidence to put her out of business.

As I looked at my two mill dogs, Mully on the chair watching TV and Thorp begging for a snack, I held them both and said, "You have both survived such adversity."

I couldn't help but take a deep breath and reflect on how strong and forgiving dogs were. All animals were. Later, I took all my dogs out and just looked at them basking in the sunlight. People have this idea of a perfect dog. They want a certain size, a certain color, and a certain personality. And so, the breeding began. When the mass marketing of dogs became very profitable, uncaring people got involved, and we were faced with puppy mills.

I had never understood the concept of a perfect dog. Buddy pretty much fell into our laps. I picked Digger and Sadie from a small icon on

Petfinder.com. When I met them and found they were nothing like their picture or description, it didn't matter. I already felt a bond. Thorp was anything but perfect, and yet he changed my life.

I have always looked past color, size, breed. I see an animal's soul. To me, any dog has the potential to be a perfect dog.

There is irony in humans demanding perfection from dogs when, in truth, humans are the most flawed species of all.

CHAPTER 30

BAD PRESS

It had been six months, and I was still fighting my paper for a story. There had been a nice story on adopting animals, so I decided to compliment the reporter and see where that could lead.

This was her response:

Ladies:

Thank you so much for the note. I've spent the past few days trying to figure out how I could do the story you have asked for.

I, too, share your distaste for the puppy-mill system. And I agree that it's a story that should be told.

However, it's not a story that I can do with the limited resources that I have. We are a local paper, focused on McHenry County. I cannot justify sending a reporter to a site north of Eau Claire, Wis., to do the story about

Thorp. It's just not feasible for us.

I hope that you can understand my dilemma. I will do all that I can reasonably do.

If your organization plans an event locally, please let me know, and I'll be more than happy to help!

Kathy Williams
Community editor
Northwest Herald

My response:

Dear Kathy,

I appreciate your concern and your personal distaste for puppy mills . . . Is there no way for the NW Herald to use my story? Or what if we were able to collect individuals or shelters in the county who have taken in puppy-mill dogs? I mean, just because the auction doesn't take place in our county does not mean that the county is not affected by these mill dogs.

There are stories right here in the county about these dogs . . . and there are so many opportunities to present them –

especially with the presidential election at hand.

In all honesty, does any of the paper's inability to do a story on this issue come from the fact that places like Petland advertise in the NW Herald? I mean, it is obvious that there is a conflict of interest . . .

Well, I will keep brainstorming. I can't give up because the truth needs to be told and the poor dogs in those horrendous conditions deserve better.

It is disheartening to find that your local paper can't think on a more national level when it comes to an issue as sad and cruel as puppy mills.

Her response:

Ms. Monroe:

To tell a fair and balanced story about the mills, I would have to have a reporter actually GO to one. Despite our feelings about the mill, I am required to be FAIR to all parties concerned. What they are doing is disgusting but it's not illegal.

In the 18 years that I've been here, I have NEVER been told not to do a story based on our advertisers. Frankly, it's insulting to even suggest it.

And there are many, many local stories that need telling, too. It's a balancing act.

If I can figure out a way to do it, I will. And I am sincerely sorry to disappoint you.

Kathy Williams
Community editor
Northwest Herald

I wanted to reply—to say something nasty, but luckily a friend stopped by before I hit send. When I went back later to send the e-mail, I realized it would be better to just let it go.

It was unbearably frustrating to see a story with so much information to support it and have a paper say that there was nothing they could do to report it.

A few days went by, and I got an e-mail from Kathy, saying she had found a way to get the story out. Another editor was going to interview me for the "Get to Know Someone in McHenry County" column.

I was on cloud nine. It was my chance to speak, to tell everyone what I knew about the mills, the pet stores, etc. . . . .

I had the interview over the phone. It became painfully obvious why I was a writer. As a writer, I could control the story and had the power to tell what I thought was important. As the interviewee, I was powerless. I hated it. She started with my favorite book, movie, etc. None of that was important. I only wanted to talk about one thing: puppy mills.

She asked questions about the auction and the mills, but I could sense that she didn't understand them well enough, or maybe she didn't even believe in them enough to get it right and print it correctly.

She asked about my local involvement with the county shelter . . . and then, finally, asked me what I most wanted to tell the readers. So, I went on and on, saying, "People should not buy dogs from a pet store. 100 percent of the dogs at a pet store are from puppy mills. If people worry that if they don't buy the dogs, they will die, then they can rest assured that if everyone stopped buying those dogs, rescues would come and save them. People should not buy dogs through websites. (This does not include www.petfinder.com, where people can locate animals needing homes through rescues and shelters.) They should always make sure that they go to the breeder's home and physically see the mother and father."

And then I said, "People should not believe that the AKC paper means anything. It is just a piece of paper that states who the mom and dad are of their puppy. It does not guarantee that they are healthy or that they were raised in a clean, loving environment."

By the end, I was breathless. I hung up the phone and felt depleted. I had had such high hopes. I wondered how it would all come out in print.

The next day, the photographer came to take a picture for the story. She was very sincere, and I could sense immediately that she got it. She asked better questions than the reporter had, and wanted the picture to portray the two mills dogs as survivors.

The Sunday paper finally came and on the front page, in big bold letters, was my name, "Pet Lover—Becky Monroe works to rescue canines from puppy mills."

A few pages back was the picture of Mully, Thorp and me . . . and as I frantically skimmed the story, I realized immediately that NONE of the pet-store information was included, none of the AKC stuff, NONE of the stuff that mattered to me. She did include my description of the auctions, but NO connection to the pet stores. Not one word.

Friends would stop me and tell me that they liked the story—that it provided good insight to people who didn't know about puppy mills.

But it could have been so much better. I felt betrayed. Were those weekly full-page ads Petland's insurance policy against bad publicity? Why was I having such a difficult time exposing the truth?

CHAPTER 31

AFFECTION

The country was about to embark on one of the most important elections of all time: Barack Obama, a black man for president, and Sarah Palin, a white woman, for vice president. They were on two different tickets that each represented different values and strategic plans. So many people are against government regulations. It's not that I believed the government should tell everyone how to run their businesses, but it sure was scary when they didn't step in to regulate them.

For years, business forced long hours on young children in unsafe work areas. When that was regulated, businesses failed to uphold environmental standards until the EPA and OSHA stepped in. Regardless of whether people wanted the government to regulate things, the truth was that unless they did, greed propelled commerce, and we were left with industries as cruel and heartless as puppy mills.

It was election night, and we went as a family to vote. As a nine-year-old, Abby had a lot of questions. Especially since her stepdad and I voted for two different candidates. She wanted to know what prompted our decisions.

I explained that it's important in life to figure out what matters to you. I said, "Once you know what matters, you can use that to guide everything you do, including who you vote for in an election."

She knew how important ending puppy mills was to me, and so she asked, "Does that mean Barack Obama will end the mills?"

I said, "His record of voting shows that he's more responsive to changing laws to protect animals than John McCain. So, I do believe that the end of puppy mills is much more possible under an Obama administration."

I admit this was a tough election. Neither candidate offered everything I wanted for my country. But a friend once told me that it is important to think with your heart and to feel what is right to you. She said, "You have to know your ideals and stick to them."

She was right. Regardless of other issues, animal welfare would always be important to me, and so that was one of my main criteria in voting for all of the candidates. I could only have faith that I was right in my choices.

During our political conversation with Abby, we also explained the evolution of our country. We told her how there was a time when women could not vote or hold certain professions. We told her how not that many years ago, people of color could not vote. Even for me, it was hard to imagine those things. I hoped one day we, as a society, would look back at factory farming and puppy mills and have a hard time imagining how something so cruel could have been legal.

As I watched the results of a historic election, all four dogs were romping around the room. Mully was the craziest. He ran and played as though he were a puppy for the first time. All of a sudden, he came over to me and started jumping, with his front paws on my knees. He let me pick him up, and then he cuddled up with me on my lap.

He was instantly calm and relaxed. It was then I realized that I had been assuming Mully didn't want cuddle time. I thought he was more interested in playing and being his own dog, so I gave him his freedom. But I had overlooked the fact that he just didn't know how to have a relationship with a human being.

His running and jumping and chewing were his defense mechanisms for not understanding how to interact with me. It was a way for him to not have to deal with rejection or his fear of people. But, really, he wanted that interaction . . . he was craving it.

It was exactly two months since the auction. Mulligan still looked at me with questioning eyes—still unsure of what human contact was. I sensed that he wanted to trust me, and he wanted me to pet him and love him; he just didn't understand what love was. He had never had anyone love him. Instead, he was born into a cage. I am sure he was too young when his mother was ripped apart from him. Soon after, his siblings would have been taken away and sent to other mills or pet stores. He would have sat alone in a rusty crate. People might have come and filled his water or food, but that was all he would have known.

Suddenly, one day, he was shipped to another state, from Oklahoma to Iowa . . . another cage, another mill. Nothing was familiar to him, and no one spoke softly to him or petted him or did anything to calm his fears. After a few months in Iowa, he found himself in Thorp, Wisconsin, at an auction. In another cage, in another barn with other dogs . . . Numerous strangers poked and prodded him in his cage. His big brown eyes opened wide and filled with fear. He scurried from one side of the cage to another, doing all he could to avoid human contact.

But now, there he was, breathing slowly, relaxing with me on the sofa. Enjoying life the way it should be for a dog. The way it should be for ALL dogs. The way it should have been from the beginning.

How miraculous that Thorp was on one side of me and Mulligan was on the other. It was less than a year ago that both dogs were lying in cages. No one cared about them. No one loved them. In fact, neither knew what it was like to be petted, to have a warm bed, or to have a family. Millions of dogs are left to live their lives alone. They are hungry and alone. They are cold and alone. They are in pain and alone, and sadly, they die alone.

Obama won the election. Abby asked, "Mom, are you happy? Does that mean the end of puppy mills?"

I always admired her innocence and her hopefulness.

"Well, I don't think it's that simple. It'll take a lot more people taking a stand and demanding justice for any president to change things. I just hope when thousands of people scream, Obama will listen."

It was hard to hear my own words because I knew, too well, they were the truth. It would take an army to win our battle.

CHAPTER 32

THE DEBATE

The debate about rescuing puppy-mill dogs at the auctions became more and more complex. Many believed that we weren't doing any good. Many felt we were only putting money in the pockets of the millers. There was little argument about the fact that we did give the millers money, and in some cases, a lot of money. At the last auction, the English bulldog who had Band-Aids covering the many open wounds on his body and his infected eyes cost the rescue over $700.

There was also the little Shih Tzu, later called Hope. She was so sick at the auction that she appeared dead. The Shih Tzu rescue paid a pretty penny to get her out because of her poor condition. It wouldn't have been humane to leave her there suffering. She was brought to a vet after the auction and was diagnosed with a severe upper respiratory infection and a bladder infection. Her small size and minimal weight made everyone believe she was a puppy, but she was an adult. She didn't have a single puppy tooth. Had she gone to another mill, she would have died.

Were we saving one and killing hundreds? Maybe. But I thought back to the rescue analogy about the starfish. There were hundreds of starfish stranded on a beach, and a little boy was throwing them back one at a time. A man walked by and said, "You will never save them all . . . why does it matter?" And the little boy replied, "It matters to the one I throw back."

When I looked at Mulligan and Thorp, saving them seemed like the only thing to do. Yes, many more were still suffering, but they were the lucky ones who were not—not anymore. As I had promised, I was using them as ambassadors for the fight against puppy mills. Just by having them in my life, hundreds of people knew about mills. Hundreds of people who previously had no idea now cared about it. Many made decisions that reflected their desire to end the plight of these dogs, and even more continued to share my story.

I believe that the dogs who are saved are the best education for the unknowing public. The dogs were the change agents. They were the only ones who could honestly represent what they had been through. Even without words, they spoke of what they had endured. Their silent scars for the entire world to see. Maybe they were unusually timid because no one had ever touched them gently. Maybe their health was bad due to the lack of veterinary care. Maybe they only had three legs because of an untreated broken bone. Maybe, like Peony, the Cavalier stitched together with wire, they actually bore scars from being sewn up like a piece of meat.

It was true that getting them out wasn't directly ending the puppy-mill industry, but each dog saved meant one fewer to breed, one fewer to sell. It wasn't the perfect answer, but it was raising the awareness level in all parts of America. Without these warriors, how would anyone understand the war we were waging?

CHAPTER 33

FOSTERING CHRISTMAS MIRACLES

There were some potential adopters interested in Mulligan. However, it was getting harder to accept that he would leave me. Knowing his days with me were numbered, I was struggling to let him go. I realized it was all part of the plan. I knew it was the right thing to do. And it allowed me the space to take in another in need of rescue.

But in just over two months, I watched him morph into a happy, loving dog. When I had met him at the auction, he had cowered in the back of the cage—afraid of any human contact. He did not know how to be petted or how to be loved. With just a few weeks of love, he was lying tightly against my body every night.

There was reward and there was sacrifice in fostering animals, and somehow, to get through, I had to accept both.

When I adopted my Maltese mix, Sadie, the person who was fostering had never done it before. Sadie was her first. She kept telling me how grateful she was that I wanted Sadie, but she also kept saying how sad she would be.

I knew I would cry when I handed Mully over to his new home. It was the right thing to do, but it would hurt like hell.

Often, people excuse themselves from the possibility of fostering because it will be too difficult to say good-bye. It is difficult. But the truth is that another animal in a shelter dies when no one is there to foster. For every pet taken out of a shelter and placed into foster care, there is room for another pet to be saved. A few tears shed when saying good-bye are a small price to pay for saving another life.

It was Christmastime, and Mulligan still needed a miracle. He had gotten a few applications for his adoption, but many were poor matches. One young woman was a great candidate, but when she went to PetSmart to get the things she would need for him, she realized how costly a dog would be, and called to let me know it wasn't a good time for her to adopt. I sincerely appreciated her honesty and her desire to provide him with a good home.

One morning, I woke to a beautiful e-mail from a couple who had devoted their lives to adopting unwanted, broken animals. They were interested in Mulligan. As the e-mail exchanges grew, it became heartwarmingly obvious that this was the perfect couple for Mulligan. They supported animal-welfare organizations wholeheartedly and wanted nothing more than to provide Mulligan with a loving home.

I called their vet, who had nothing but wonderful things to say about them. I was so excited for Mulligan. And it certainly made me reflect on the power of fate.

Just a few months ago, Mulligan had been in a puppy mill. No one wanted him. Not a single person at the whole auction. Mine was the only hand that went up when they said, "Fifty for this one."

There was no way to explain why I wanted him in objective terms. I just had a place for him in my heart.

People like me have faith in dogs. We don't pick them because they are purebreds, or the prettiest or the smartest of the litter. We don't pick them because we fall in love with them. We pick them because no one else did.

We have faith that in time, things work out. Eventually, everyone in the house learns to get along. They learn to be housetrained, or we learn how to live with it. Most of all, we allow them to grow and to flourish. Ultimately, we find that they have melted our hearts just by being the dog no one else was going to allow them to be.

I loved Mulligan. He was full of life and love and full of the dickens. I was in awe that things had worked out the way they did. He had gone unwanted his whole life.

But when Beth e-mailed me and described in detail her background and her desire to adopt Mulligan, I couldn't help but smile and be inspired. To know there actually were other people out there with the same passion and compassion for animals was truly hopeful.

CHAPTER 34

DEAF EARS

As I was working on placing Mulligan and emotionally coping with giving him up, I was also dealing, once again, with the *Northwest Herald*. New information had surfaced about Petland, so I forwarded it to my contact at the paper, Kathy. While Kathy had never actually done a story for me, she tried to put me in contact with the right people.

I wrote an editorial:

Letter to the Editor:

> As the holidays are approaching, it seems a great time to point out that latest investigation from the Humane Society of the United States which was released publicly on November 20, 2008. After an 8-month investigation, they have proven, without a doubt, that Petland DOES purchase their puppies from puppy

mills across the United States and specifically, in the Midwest.

While the holidays are a popular time to give pets, especially puppies, as gifts, please do not support businesses that buy puppy-mill dogs. I have witnessed the puppy-mill industry firsthand and it is an atrocity. Dogs lying in their feces, no socialization, with little care or shelter. Petland and pet stores like them need to adopt the philosophy of Petco and PetSmart, who support rescue and shelter groups for dog adoptions.

And, truthfully, while a puppy in a stocking is unbearably cute, think twice before giving the gift of a pet this season. A pet of any type is a lifelong commitment. But, if it is the right choice, please rescue a homeless animal from one of the many great shelters or breed rescues in McHenry County.

Deep down, I knew it would never get printed. I knew that the *Northwest Herald* valued Petland's advertising dollars far more than they valued the truth. But I kept sticking the needle in Kathy. She had said from the beginning that she really did want to help me because she loved animals.

Once I sent her the latest on Petland, I received a call from Calvin Meade, an editor. He had called me a week prior to verify my letter. I had written probably ten or so letters to the editor over the course of a few years. Every letter I had written on other topics had been verified and printed, all within no more than five days. It was interesting that the latest letter was taking so long.

Calvin and I played phone tag and then, finally, he returned my call while I was home. In about two minutes, Calvin rudely and abruptly "explained" to me that he would NEVER write anything bad about ANY local business and definitely not about Petland.

I tried to explain that this was not my opinion but general facts for the public. I asked if he could at least print the Associated Press news release on the HSUS's eight-month investigation.

"No, I gave you the parameters. It's up to you to make them work," he said.

The parameters were the whole "cannot print anything bad about a local business" bullshit. The *Northwest Herald* had done many features on local businesses that had issues. One mulching company was recycling old pallets, and their mulch for yards and playgrounds had nails in it. A local chemical company was supposedly leaking chemicals into the groundwater and causing cancer. The county nursing home was being labeled as having poor standards and being uncaring.

These were all local businesses and they all had bad press. And some of the bad press was hearsay but was still printed.

I was outraged. Here I was, placing Mulligan, reliving his sad and neglected journey, and my local paper refused to speak the truth. One look in Thorp's aged eyes, and I just couldn't stand it. Millions of dogs were suffering, the truth was staring me in the eyes, and I could not get anyone to publish it or even recognize it?

I sent an e-mail to Shaw, the company who owned the *Northwest Herald*:

> To whom this may concern:
>
> I want to relay my pure disappointment in finding out that your newspaper corporation not only fails to seek out and report the truth to the community, but also supports animal cruelty.
>
> For the last nine months I have tried to contact numerous editors at the Northwest Herald to convey the importance of exposing the truth about puppy mills to our community. I, personally, have rescued dogs directly from these mills and wanted my fellow

neighbors to know that such cruelty does exist and is having a direct effect in our community.

I was placated with a boilerplate interview in the newspaper that did not address any of the issues with local pet stores and instead focused only on my interaction at the county animal control. What mattered the most, the puppy mills and how local pet stores are involved, was left out.

In the meantime, Oprah dedicated one whole show to the topic and many follow-up episodes. She reported that she received THE most amount of viewers praise for addressing the issue, and still the NW Herald didn't feel it was a viable topic.

More recently, the Humane Society of the United States publicly reported that after an 8-month investigation, they can prove that Petland DOES sell puppies from puppy mills. In fact, the Associated Press did a news release on this topic less than a month ago.

I have tried, unsuccessfully, to get the NW Herald to report these truths in our paper – either by reporting themselves, allowing my letter to the editor to be published, or simply just reprinting the AP article. Today, I was told that they will NEVER print anything negative about Petland.

Wow, even if it is a truth? Isn't that subjective reporting? And doesn't that make quite a statement about the validity of ANY of the articles you do report on? Nonchalantly, I made the accusation months ago that the NW Herald would never say anything bad about Petland because they appear to be one of the biggest advertisers . . . One editor in particular was absolutely appalled by my statement. Yet, I find myself with nothing else to believe.

There have been numerous negative stories on other businesses in the area, why not Petland?? Sad, how very sad, that the truth loses out to money.

However, saddest of all is that in not reporting the truth, your organization is actually promoting cruelty to animals, and that is a message I think ALL of your subscribers and advertisers need to be aware of.

Across the United States, numerous referendums protecting animals and providing better animal welfare were passed in the last election. Being anti-animal isn't the popular thing to do these days and yet, Shaw seems to believe it is – all in the name of profitability.

My hope is that Shaw is not aware of the NW Herald's stand to protect Petland. I am hoping that as a corporation you have better ethics than the ones they are demonstrating.

This is not MY opinion of Petland. These are published facts about a corporation who is cruel and uncaring. I didn't buy a dog from Petland and am not looking for revenge. I have been in the trenches with the dogs who come from mills, and I have seen the facts. All I am asking is for my local paper to help educate people on what the truth is. I thought that was the intention of a newspaper.

Any responses would be greatly appreciated.

They never did respond. Not one e-mail, letter or call.

CHAPTER 35

SCREAM

I was having a hard time. Sometimes, I wished I could go back to not knowing anything about puppy mills or animal welfare. It was a more blissful, albeit ignorant life. There was just so much guilt and worry, knowing all of the horrible things being done to animals. Even worse, no matter how loudly I screamed to change things, no one heard.

I received an exciting e-mail that asked for participants for a Petland protest in Wheaton, Illinois. Ellen Holecamp, a vet tech by profession and an animal rescuer, was organizing the protest. She had heard about the Humane Society's desire to have rallies across the Unites States on Saturday, January 10. They had one planned for Naperville, and she thought the Wheaton location would also be great—with lots of traffic.

I immediately called Susan, who was just as eager to participate. This was what we were waiting for: our chance to be heard, to be seen.

The day came, and blizzard conditions couldn't stop over thirty of us die-hard dog lovers from showing the world what Petland was all about.

Deep inside, I felt like I owed it to all of the dogs in the Thorp auctions. I had never protested when I attended the auctions. This was my chance to say what my heart felt.

People drove from all over to hold signs that read, "Petland, please stop selling puppies."

We made quite an impact. Honking horns and thumbs-up from drivers all signaled that they agreed with our message. A few people even stopped to say thank you. One kind woman brought us a large container of fresh hot chocolate from Starbucks as a way to show support for the cause.

I even brought Abby along. Not only did I want one more body to hold a sign, I also wanted my daughter to know the importance of standing behind something that you believe in—something you are willing to support even when it might not be easy or popular. Seeing her hold a sign was my hopeful inspiration that future generations won't tolerate such cruelty.

The local paper, the *Wheaton Sun*, was there to get the story. Of course, I was thrilled to share my information. Susan and I explained how we had seen puppy mills and how horrible they were. We told the reporter how when you are passionate about something, no weather can stop you. We commented on how these were the types of conditions the mill dogs were living in, so it was only fair that we endure them for a few hours to get the message across.

I was so happy to see a local paper reporting on the story—being willing to expose the truth about Petland's puppies.

The two Petland stores in Illinois we protested that day were ones that HSUS had investigated, and had found proof that they were buying from mills. The truth was slowly starting to come out, and it was stunning those who didn't know.

A few days after the protest, the story was printed in the *Wheaton Sun*. Pictures of the protestors lined the story, and I was quoted on my experience at the Thorp auctions. It was validating to be heard.

CHAPTER 36

A FAMILY TO LOVE

It was a blizzardy day, and it was tempting to cancel Mulligan's transport to his new home in Madison, Wisconsin. It would be the last day he would snuggle up with me. But, right away in the morning, Beth called to say that they were so excited to welcome Mully and hoping I could still make the trip.

I knew it was now or maybe never. It was time to say good-bye, and time for Mulligan to start his real second chance.

He sat in the front seat on his favorite blanket, as though he were my copilot on the trip to his new home. The roads were treacherous, but I was delivering a Christmas miracle.

When I arrived at Beth and John's, I was greeted by their family, which consisted of many dogs, including a blind Shih Tzu wearing a sweater. They were proud to show me where all the dogs ate, and the many different kinds of food they used to satisfy varying needs. There were dog beds throughout the house, and there was one bedroom designated just for the dogs.

Mulligan had come to the right place. Within minutes, the others were chasing him. He was wagging his tail and chasing back. Beth and John were elated. Mulligan had found his family. He was home.

I backed out of the driveway and couldn't help but cry. It was a pivotal moment for me. It was the first time I had personally rescued a dog and found him a home. I had single-handedly changed a dog's life. It was overwhelming.

It was a three-hour drive back home in the snow, and all I could do was relive the last nine months of my life. The two auctions, Mulligan, Thorp, my battles with the paper and speaking the truth. I had learned so much about life, and in the process, a metamorphosis had occurred: I was braver, louder, stronger. A single event had changed everything I knew about myself and the world I lived in. I would never be the same and I didn't want to be. It was freeing to be a part of a cause—to fight for something I believed in.

When I arrived home, I opened an e-mail from one of the rescuers, filled with pictures of the goldendoodle I had purchased at the September auction. I found out that it was actually the second time she had been auctioned off. I remember taking my paperwork to her cage and looking into the blank stare in her eyes. She lay still and frozen with no intent to get out of the cage, her fur matted and her body shaking. She had no idea what her fate would be.

I had to physically pull her out of the cage. She wouldn't walk on the leash. With Mulligan in my arms, it was all I could do to have her follow me. I remember placing her in Shayla's car. My heart broken, knowing that she had been bred for four years so that unknowing consumers could boast about their own goldendoodle puppies in a city park or obedience class. She had never been to a park or obedience school. She had never seen the light of day, but her puppies probably sold for well over $1000 each.

The e-mail was to let us all know that Crystal, as she had been named, was adopted by her foster home. Attached to the e-mail were pictures of Crystal with her new siblings, and I could finally see a spark in her eyes as she cuddled close with a family she could call her own. She had a real home now.

That was what it was all about. The thousands of dogs, prisoners of greed, who deserved more. Mulligan, Crystal, Hope, Peony, Thorp and so many more whom we had saved and given names were living in homes, making people happy. They finally had families to love them.

The journey was painstaking. Every step, every letter, every call, every tear shed; but seeing pictures of dogs who now had lives outside of metal cages with light in their eyes made it all worth it.

CHAPTER 37

GETTING LOUDER

As I was spending time trying to convince my local paper to run a story about the truth behind pet-store windows and the glaring reality of puppy mills, I was contacted by a Wisconsin paper, the *Isthmus*, which was looking to do a piece on the auctions and the people who rescue the dogs.

Linda Falkenstein wanted to report the truth, and she wanted to get the story out before the March auction, with the intent of getting more people out to see what was really going on.

I was thrilled. Linda and I set up a conference call, and I was able to share everything I knew. Her story would detail the exploitation of dogs in Wisconsin and shine a light on how such practices were legal in the state. She interviewed all of the people I had come to know—all of them working hard to put an end to the plight of the dogs. Our voices were being called on, and people wanted to listen.

Linda's story was heartfelt and called out the atrocities of puppy mills and their prevalence in Wisconsin and other parts of the United States. She reported all that we told her. What hit closest for me was that she believed us. It was unlike my dealings with my local paper—she was willing to go against the mainstream and report the truth.

It was affirming to know that the truth still mattered.

CHAPTER 38

SADLY FAMILIAR

On March 11, 2009, I attended my third auction. This time, I had a designated mission: I knew which dogs from the dreaded auction list I would save. I had raised money by begging friends and family, and I knew I would get six dogs out.

Five of them were Chinese crested powder puffs. They were all from the same litter, only seven months old. When I saw them on the list, I was immediately taken. A year ago, a four-and-a-half-year-old male Chinese crested powder puff had stolen my heart and changed my life.

There was no doubt that I would have to get those five pups out. It was my responsibility. Knowing that the Chinese Crested Rescue and Elmbrook Humane would help foster and place them, I also knew that I personally would have to choose another dog who needed me. Another dog whom I would foster and place as a small part of my contribution to save the world, or at least educate people around me about the horror behind pet-store windows that they never see.

When the auction list came out, as every time before, I was sickened and heartbroken. The list made it all so real and all too horrible. Hundreds of dogs listed as though they were soulless. As though they had no beating heart or wagging tail, they were listed like commodities, not pets.

As with the auctions before, I stared at the list when it came out. I tried to picture each of the dogs and then, like before, I felt that lump in my throat. The lump that reminded me: none of these dogs realized that their fate was about to change, maybe for the better or maybe for the worse.

I hated that these innocent creatures were forced to be dependent on people who had no regard for their loyalty, their compassion and their unending desire to please. They were nothing to these people, and yet they were everything to me—to every rescuer who cried at the list and agonized over whom to save and what it would take to end the travesty.

The list was long and sad, and so I left the decision of which dog to choose to a dear friend of mine, Ellen. We had become friends while volunteering at our local animal control.

Within minutes, she picked one of the oldest dogs on the list. A four-and-a-half-year-old female Shih Tzu whose listing read, "Good mother, in heat next week."

Undoubtedly, the poor dog had been bred often and certainly needed a way out. Without knowing any more, I knew she was the one for me.

In the field of animal rescue, I had learned to believe in the impossible. No matter how my own faith teetered, I had to keep convincing myself that every step, every word was making a difference. Too many days were filled with anguish and pain, and too few were filled with reward and accomplishment. Saving one dog at a time was torture—especially when there were so many more out there who needed saving.

I went in with all of my heart, ready to change the world, and in a short time, I realized that I could not. It felt devastating and depleting. I had to believe that choosing one to rescue was enough, because that was all I could do.

The drive, the protestors outside, the parking lot and the walk into the auction barn had become all too familiar to me. I was numb to all of it.

The day was bleak and unbearably cold. Thirty-five degrees below zero with the windchill. The inside of the barn was even colder. Contrary to the rumors before the auction that the dogs would be healthier and better cared for to show that the millers were cleaning up their act, they were huddled in the backs of the wire cages, many of them matted, ill, and bearing obvious scars of being bred again and again.

An English bulldog had a Band-Aid on to hide a horrible, infected wound. The Band-Aid eventually fell off, as did many of the masks the puppy-mill people hid behind. Looking at the numerous cages and seeing the ugly truth glaring at me left me empty.

The crowd was huge. If anyone looked closely, they would have seen that many in the crowd were rescuers, and of those, many were there for the first time. It was easy to spot them; they were the ones wiping tears from their eyes and desperately looking around in the hopes that there were other people just like them.

I remembered feeling like that a year ago. I remembered holding my breath and wiping tears. I remembered being completely aghast at what I was seeing. I mostly remembered feeling very alone.

But this time, I had come with three other people. Margie and Susan returned, and Jodi joined us—her first auction. I found myself saying hi to many people I knew and introducing myself to others, somehow managing a smile when I recognized a face. The turnout was much higher than at the other auctions, and the viewing area became quite crowded with onlookers. The irony of all of us being jammed in the very area where dogs lived like that every day. It was also the first time that the Mennonite and Amish people were outnumbered by people like us.

It was our true hope that this would be the last auction we would ever have to attend in Wisconsin.

Legislation was fast accelerating, and rumors spread that this could be the end.

I was focused on finding the Chinese cresteds and the Shih Tzu I had promised to myself I would save. I found the cresteds: the three females cramped in one crate and the two males in the other. All five huddled in the battered crates, matted, skinny and exuding stench. But I was also busy connecting to other rescuers who, through e-mail, had befriended me.

I made my way to the little Shih Tzu, #106. Just like the CCs, she was matted and slumped in the corner, completely exposed to the whole audience. She was white with gray ears and a large gray spot that resembled the shape of a heart. She was caged with other Shih Tzus, and all the Shih Tzus were in the center of the viewing area. Each walked on metal wires, doing anything they could to avoid eye contact.

There were a lot of lifeless dogs, and many wore the scars of forced and repeated motherhood—many with engorged nipples, and others with their raw teats dragging across the rusty chicken-wire floor, too overused to tighten up ever again.

As with my previous two auctions, two dogs would stand out: two Shih Tzus that I couldn't save. Like the beagles at the first auction and the Yorkies at the second, the Shih Tzus haunted me. Shaved down to their bare skin and absolutely petrified in their cage.

It was sad to have become a part of the underground world of puppy-mill auctions. I found myself in what was now familiar territory: the harsh reality of dog breeding. A reality too few would ever come to understand.

But, however unfortunate the situation, there was comfort in knowing I had become part of a strong force. There were many of us, bonded by a desire to not just save as many dogs as we could on that frigid day, but to find a way to end the business altogether.

Our force wasn't just comprised of people inside, looking frantically into cages of despair. There was an entire army of protestors outside. They were letting others know that it was wrong and horrible. The protestors held the line outside for over six hours in the nearly unbearable cold, all in the name of expressing what was going on inside the auction barn. I remember one of them coming to get some reprieve from the cold and saying to me, "My heart is in here, my head is out there."

For weeks prior to the auction, many rescuers felt they wouldn't be able to rescue due to lack of funds or a personal conflict with contributing to the business; but on the day of the auction, 70 percent of the dogs went to rescue. I think it is easy to say you can't rescue any until you get there and your heart breaks, and any type of reasoning falls apart.

Proud and relieved, we loaded vans and cars and trucks with frightened dogs. It was a rush to be part of something amazing. It was a miracle to the dogs who got out. The ones who would find a new home, a cozy blanket to sleep on, and a loving family to finally call their own.

But beyond the fear of looking back and watching a handful of innocent pups in a Mennonite's arms, each with slightly wagging tails, trusting of what will happen to them next . . . was the gut-wrenching fact: we had just contributed to their profit and helped propel the very business we despised.

And that was where I found myself: completely torn and disheartened.

Weeks prior, fellow rescuers had attended an auction in Missouri. They came back with many dogs and reported to us some of the saddest news I had heard. Many of the dogs they bought went for under five dollars. And there were a bunch of dogs whom they purchased for A PENNY each. A penny for a life—a soul with a wagging tail.

I realized people gave away dogs for free, but seeing a dog sold in an auction for a penny only demonstrated how little value these loving creatures had to the people in the business. A penny screamed, "This animal is worthless."

To buy or not to buy wasn't really the question. The only question that remained was: What would it take for both legislators and their constituents to believe what we had witnessed?

I had taken six dogs out the day of my third auction. The five Chinese crested powder puffs were divided up by the shelters who would take them. Two went to Elmbrook Humane, the shelter of my very first auction friend, Carol. It was hard to believe that I had met her only a year ago. It felt like a lifetime.

Two others went to Clark County Humane. When we left the barn, we drove straight there. The shelter was full of people crying over the auction. Many of them had never been to an auction before and were heartbroken after witnessing it firsthand. In their loving arms were the lucky dogs who got out on that frigid day. Dogs who would see vets, feel warmth and eventually have a permanent place to call home.

There was magic at the shelter that day. Amid the tears and the pain was an overwhelming sense of love—thanks to so many, dogs were free. Literally. We had physically taken dogs out of a bad situation and given them a second chance. Some might think only people of great power can change the world. But the truth is, anybody can—we did on that cold day in March.

The last Chinese crested powder puff made the drive with me and went to the Chinese Crested Rescue—the same rescue Thorp was supposed to go to a year earlier.

Even after having done it before, it was still hard for me to describe what it was like to drive with two unknown dogs in the back of my car. Two dogs I had never seen before. Two dogs without names. Two dogs whose destiny I held in my hands. I cherished the opportunity to change their lives.

CHAPTER 39

STRONGER, TOUGHER

The four-and-a-half-year-old Shih Tzu I saved became Penelope. Named by my husband—who a year ago had wanted nothing to do with a mill dog.

I questioned if I would be able to adopt her to anyone but myself. Regardless of her past, she was the happiest little dog I had ever met. Her first few days with us, she was cautious. She would shake often. Like Thorp and Mulligan, grass was unfamiliar to her, and stairs were unimaginable. When I would go to pet her or pick her up, she would bolt across the room. Humans hadn't been her friends. But she had a spark to her. She was stronger, tougher than she seemed at first glance.

I was stronger and tougher, too. A year ago, I had brought home Thorp, with no idea how to care for him. Now I was looking into the eyes of a little Shih Tzu, 365 days later, and I wasn't afraid or unsure. I knew the next steps; I knew what I needed to do for her. I had grown more in twelve months than I had in thirty years.

Still, I paused to imagine what her life had been like . . . She was my first female mill dog. The physical impact on the females is much more evident. Her nipples were enlarged, her paws were so matted that I couldn't even see the pads or the nails, and her teeth looked like someone had glued concrete to them. When she was spayed, the vet told me that her little uterus all but fell out—he had never seen anything so awful before. To imagine that kind of neglect and to realize how resilient she was gave me hope that her future would be bright.

Most of all, to see her lie snuggled up against me as I slept was a deep-seated reminder that dogs were not things or machines. They were little souls who longed to be loved and who deserved, at the very least, respect and dignity.

Stuffing them in wire crates, in both frigid and scorching temperatures, and literally ripping out their offspring and selling them under false pretenses was plainly and simply WRONG.

All of my life, I had maintained a positive outlook. A never-ending belief that things would get better in time. However, in just one year, all of my beliefs about all people being inherently good had failed me. No good people treated animals that way, and no good government sat back and watched it.

The world had evolved. It was time to end the suffering for the dogs, and it was time for all of us to become compassionate, humane beings.

CHAPTER 40

DEMOCRACY

On March 31, 2009, Susan and I made our way to the state capitol in Madison, Wisconsin, to attend Humane Lobby Day, sponsored by HSUS. The main agenda was to speak with our local legislators about the two bills aimed at puppy-mill regulation.

At the opening remarks, I was asked by the local TV station, NBC15 WMTV, for an interview on what I had experienced that compelled me to attend Lobby Day. I was crazy nervous when they said it would air on the ten o'clock news. I had ten minutes to prepare myself. I had so much to say. Fortunately, the woman who interviewed me asked the questions which allowed me to say what I knew needed to be addressed.

I got to show a picture of Thorp and to tell a brief part of his story. I felt like I was able to make the smallest contribution to the betterment of dogs in Wisconsin. I was finding my voice, and with courage fueled solely by my passion for the subject, I was talking to hundreds, probably thousands or possibly even tens of thousands of people about what I had experienced.

I was afraid, but I was facing my fears because I knew I was right. I knew that the dogs needed a voice, and for some reason, I was the one people were listening to, even if it was only for three minutes on the nightly news.

I saw the clip later the following day. There I was, holding a photo of Thorp and me. Telling our story and the stories of others. They included the conditions of the dogs I described, and they used the part where I said the dogs didn't know what human touch was. While I was always left with the desire for more to be covered in interviews, I was satisfied, and there was affirmation in making the ten o'clock news.

We were there because we had faced the auctions, we had seen what Wisconsin was up against, and we had rescued dogs from the poorest conditions allowed in the state. Susan and I were from Illinois, but to our advantage, we both owned homes in Wisconsin—which meant we felt we had every right to address our local legislators about the issues. We might not get to vote, but we did pay the taxes that paid their salaries. We felt justified.

We found our legislators and went in to plead our case. We had our experiences to share. The first thing we were met with was distaste for HSUS. It was as though we should have removed our HSUS Lobby Day buttons to be heard. But once we explained our personal version of what we had seen and told the stories of the dogs we had rescued, Senator Luther Olsen and his chief of staff listened intently.

We left our meeting feeling good—feeling proud that we had come to the capitol and contributed to the true democracy our country was founded for. As constituents, we did our civic duty; we spoke our piece and hoped that our words, our truths would change the fate of innocent dogs in Wisconsin.

Weeks later, Susan and I made a second whirlwind trip to the capitol in Madison. We had heard that the bills were about to be released to the press, as it was going to a public hearing. We wanted to be there because to us, the day was monumental. It meant more to me than I had even imagined—it was everything I was fighting for.

The bills to be known as AB 250 in the Assembly and SB 208 in the Senate were introduced by Representative Jeff Smith and Senator Pat Kreitlow, and had been drafted by a committee made up of various animal-welfare representatives such as: Chuck Wegner, the executive director of Clark County Humane, the county where the Thorp auction took place; Eilene Ribbens, the executive director of the No Wisconsin Puppy Mills organization; and Wisconsin State Veterinarian Dr. Yvonne Bellay. I knew each of them.

A previous bill had failed to get to the floor for a vote before the congressional session for 2008 ended, and the bill was dropped. Our only hope was that the new committee would act fast and draft bills to be introduced and passed quickly before the end of 2009.

The new bills placed a specific limit on how many dogs could be adopted, sold or transferred at twenty-five per year. The bills, unlike others introduced before it, targeted not only mass breeding facilities such as puppy mills and backyard breeders, but rescues and shelters as well. Because shelters and rescues would be required to operate under the same regulations, it had the potential to be more widely accepted by the breeders' associations and sporting-dog groups.

There was some backlash from the animal-welfare community, which argued that they were all nonprofit organizations without the funds to operate as breeding facilities did, but the legislature made no changes to the bills.

One of the issues rescues had going against them was that a local group operating under the guise of a shelter was raided, and numerous puppies were found in bad health and in poor conditions. The woman who ran the organization known as Thyme and Sage Ranch, Jennifer Petkus, said that she was saving dogs from Amish puppy millers and finding them good homes.

However, unlike a reputable rescue, she was not medically treating the animals. She was not getting them spayed or neutered and not getting them groomed—she was basically acting like a broker and turning the dogs over for a profit.

Friends of mine from the Wisconsin Rescue Platform, as we called ourselves, had seen Petkus at the auctions, and many had seen the bad conditions her dogs were in. Members of the group, including myself, reported her to Petfinder.com. We believed that she was portraying herself as a rescuer, when in reality, she was just selling the dogs the Amish millers would give her. She was removed from Petfinder.

The American Society for the Prevention of Cruelty to Animals (ASPCA) investigated her, and over three hundred animals were seized from her property. Eventually, she went to trial and was convicted on six counts of animal cruelty. She served as animal control and the dog pound for Richland County, so, as with any political circus, the county was reluctant to shut her down.

In the end, justice won and Petkus was put out of business. The Dane County Humane Society was flooded with all of Petkus's dogs but found permanent homes or foster homes for all of them.

As we ran up the steps to the capitol and listened to Senator Pat Kreitlow and Representative Jeff Smith talk about the bills, my heart opened—

maybe for the first time in months. I didn't feel the ache any longer: I felt the hope. Hope that all of the anguish I had endured and all of the suffering the dogs had survived meant something. We were being heard—we were really being heard.

The TV stations were there capturing every word, and when the residents of Wisconsin tuned into the evening news, they would hear a reality that many never even knew existed. Hopefully, their eyes would widen and their ears would perk up and they would be informed of the travesty in their state. They would talk the next day at the water cooler and ask each other what a puppy mill was. They would start to look at pet stores differently and question why they didn't adopt their last dog.

For a few brief moments, my heart was full of hope that a mere press release would change everything.

Until it became obvious that not everyone in the audience was there to support the bills. There were dog "ownership" groups who would fight for their right to "own" a dog the way they wanted to. They would fight to keep dogs as property, not as pets. There were bad breeders opposing the bills because they would cut into their profits to supply their dogs with basic needs like nutritious food and vet care.

Hunters fought the bills because to them, they would be intrusive to their hobby.

My small glimmer of hope was short-lived, and I began to realize that the fight had really just begun.

CHAPTER 41

I WANT ONE LIKE THAT

One day, Thorp, Penelope and I went for a walk and ran into some neighbors who were astounded by the changes in the dogs. They couldn't believe how healthy they looked and how happy they appeared to be. One said, "They're like real dogs now."

I couldn't stop myself. "They were always real dogs."

The other neighbor said, "I want to get a little dog just like that one," pointing to Penelope.

I explained how many dogs there were just like Penelope in rescues and shelters, but I don't think she really heard me. It was hard for me to comprehend. It was as though they could not make the connection between the two dogs standing before them and the idea that there were thousands of dogs waiting for a home like one of theirs in the suburbs.

I couldn't help but swallow hard, realizing that what I spent so much time immersed in was what so many others didn't even question.

For them it was simple—dogs like Penelope were cute and they wanted one. And for me, nothing could have seemed farther from the truth.

CHAPTER 42

UNITED FRONT

Susan and I made our way to the hearing at the capitol. It was nearly the same day of what would have been the auction in September, but for the first time, there wouldn't be an auction in September because of growing public awareness and the mounting pressure from the proposed bills. At the capitol, there was a gathering of animal people from all over the state, representing groups from across the spectrum: from animal rights to animal owners, breeders and canine registries. Hunters and vegans and everything in between. Everyone piled into the hall and waited to see what would happen.

There was a rumor that even the most vehemently opposed animal groups such as sportsmen's groups (groups who had historically challenged bills because they believed they eliminated "ownership" rights) were going to support the bill. But after ten years of trying, no one was taking anything for granted. Everyone needed to hear it for themselves.

So many of the same people who would have been huddled outside of the Thorp auction barn protesting were seated next to each other; rescuers who were once crying, silently visiting one caged dog after another, fearing they wouldn't be able to take enough home, were riding the elevator together, looking forward to entering a room as a united group.

The people I had met just two years ago surrounded me, and like the first time I met them, I found myself grateful to be with them, to know them, to be a part of them.

We had done this. Not alone, of course, but our stories, our sagas, our dogs had told the state and the country what was going on. It wasn't a secret anymore. We had made a difference.

The hearing lasted all day. And for 90 percent of it, group upon group was coming forward to testify in support of the bills. There were a few groups and individuals who were opposed. One, of course, was America's Pet Registry—who would go bankrupt without the thousands of mill dogs produced each year. And there were a few less educated, less caring breeders who spoke only of the money they would lose if these regulations took effect. Even the not-so-pro-animal state leaders could read between their words.

The support was overwhelming—even the owner groups and the hunting groups and the antigovernment groups agreed that this was good legislation. It was a day of success—real success. All of the dogs who had given their lives reveled silently as they looked down upon us.

All of the dogs fortunate enough to have been rescued wagged their tails, and all of the dogs yet to be freed let their souls smile for the first time. I could feel it all.

This was the beginning of the end.

CHAPTER 43

AKC – ACT II

I had been contemplating all that had happened in the last few months and the last few years since I exposed myself to the atrocity of puppy mills, and found myself once again angry with the AKC.

If only they would crack down—if only they would care. I couldn't get it out of my mind that if the AKC would take responsibility and assume some sense of accountability for all of this, things would get better even without the legislation.

And so, I wrote again to the organization:

> I appreciate your rather quick reply and find it intriguing that you state your support of anti-cruelty laws. When, in fact, the AKC is one of the leading dog groups to lobby against anti puppy-mill bills.
>
> Case in point is the recent legislation in WI – SB208 and AB250, which have been in the

senate and the assembly the month of October and passed unanimously in the senate in November.

However, as the bills approached the floors, memos from the AKC lobbied against the bills. Bills that would protect animals from neglect and cruelty – issues you stated the AKC supports – and yet, the AKC was unable to support these two specific bills.

For over 10 years the state of WI has been working towards this type of legislation, and when the bills passed through the general assembly, the AKC made a mass effort to stop the progress of bills that would only improve the lives of millions of dogs in WI, as well as help set the stage for many other states to follow suit.

After being present at the public hearing of the bills, I know, without hesitation, that every major dog group came forward and supported the bills as amended. This included groups like the WI Dog Federation, an "owners" group who vigilantly was against the bills when they were introduced but by a member vote chose to support the bills.

The only group who came forward against the bills was the America's Pet Registry, Inc. Is it coincidence that both the APRI and the AKC would protest these bills? I think not. Both organizations profit from mass breeding facilities because for each dog born, a registration fee is paid to one of the groups . . . If mass-breeding facilities decreased in numbers, so would the profitability of the AKC and the APRI.

It is simple numbers, and with both organizations publicly demonstrating against bills like these, it is sadly obvious as to why. It is not about protecting animals from cruelty, it is about increasing profitability.

Isn't that why the AKC has recently developed registration for mixed breeds? Another opportunity to exploit unknowing consumers and innocent dogs.

While it is apparent what side I have taken, I am still quite interested in learning the reasoning for the AKC's adamant disapproval of legislation designed to protect dogs, to prevent cruelty and to promote good breeding practices.

I do believe that when the AKC was founded, its intent was to insure the health, temperament and lineage of the breed, as well as to support the good breeders whose interest in the canines was solely to progress the breed out of pride and passion.

Sadly, today, the AKC has turned toward profitability instead of integrity.

Hopefully, as bills manage to pass and the horror of puppy mills is ended and the crass stores like Petland are exposed – the AKC will be left with very little. In fact, if the good breeders get smart – they, too, should abandon the organization because it chose to forsake them in the pursuit of greed.

They never responded.

CHAPTER 43

HOPE

On December 1, 2009, AB 250 and SB 208 were signed into law by Governor Jim Doyle. They had passed through all of the committees and both houses with unanimous votes.

Things would not change overnight—there was still a lot of work to be done. Committees to form, investigators and inspectors to train, laws to implement. It would all take time, but the reality was that Wisconsin had taken a stand against puppy mills; and already, with a no-show auction in September, things were looking brighter.

The law stair-stepped into effect over time . . . but already, my group of rescuers was diligently working to develop anonymous relations with the millers. It was important the millers remained anonymous because if we gave away their identities when we took their dogs, they would stop contacting us. Relationships would be fostered with trust and honesty. No longer trying to prove a point or tell a story with the dogs, we were just trying to save them.

The millers were closing up shop, and they were willing to practically give the dogs away. Some of the puppies came with a small price tag of around ten to twenty-five dollars each, but the older dogs were free, and the millers were dumping them in bunches.

As the good news spread and the laws took effect, my efforts came to a close. I stayed involved with rescuing the dogs in northwestern Wisconsin, and I stayed involved with the original group I had become a part of and felt proud to know. And I certainly would stay on top of the state legislation and federal rulings and do whatever I could to express my beliefs about the welfare of animals. That ran thick in my veins.

But the truth was that it was my time to move forward, to take a deep breath and sigh—to realize that I, one person, had helped to make a difference. Not just in the lives of a few dogs, but in the lives of many. I was able to find the courage to tell my story, to tell Mulligan's story, Penelope's story, the many dogs' stories I had learned through my rescue friends, and mostly, I have told Thorp's story. Little #171, who for whatever reason spoke to me in a way that I couldn't resist, and who changed my life.

While the hard battles faded, a new chapter of the story began. In January 2010, Thorp took a class to become a therapy dog and to earn his Canine Good Citizen award. Besides knowing from day one that

Thorp had a special place in my world, I learned that he had his own special place in the world—helping others overcome their difficulties.

Thorp has an almost unimaginable heart. His eyes demonstrate an understanding that anything is possible if you just believe, and if you can find the right person to love you unconditionally. I know, now, that is all Thorp wants—to share his warmth and his soul with others. Being a therapy dog was his calling.

Thorp had what it took to become a therapy dog. He had the spirit and the unflinching kindness, but he also had to learn the basics: sit, stay, down and other commands.

Thorp had a few difficulties with the eight-week class. He was unable to lie down on command, a common problem for dogs with trust issues. Because of his attachment to me, it was nearly impossible for him to sit and stay and allow me to walk away.

Even though Thorp hadn't been successful with all of the commands, I signed us up for the test because in my heart, I knew it was the only way I would make it a priority in my life. Thorp and I had a deadline, and I would be damned if we didn't pass. I knew it was important to Thorp's well-being to share his spirit. He had come so far.

As the test approached, I got serious. Unlike with any dog I have had, I worked with Thorp three times a day on the down command and the sit-stay. We would go over the other requirements, but with unending perseverance, we worked on the main two he found almost impossible.

After a pound of liver sausage and hours of practice, the fated moment arrived, nearly two years to the day of our rescue.

I was so nervous. I kept telling myself that even if he didn't pass, it was OK. We could try again—as many times as we needed.

The day of the test, Thorp and I were walking together into a building that would change both of our lives again, for the better.

I was unable to use treats during the test, so I loaded up liver sausage under my fingernails, a trick a trainer had taught me. I had learned a lot in training with Thorp.

I remembered going to obedience school many years ago, when I got my first dog as an adult, a nine-month-old golden retriever who was returned to a breeder. Her name was Kailey, and she was a handful. I remember being in class and silently wishing for a different dog. One who sat quietly next to me—unlike Kailey, who bounced off the walls and howled. Regardless of her obnoxious behavior, I loved her.

When Thorp and I went to obedience school for the first time, I was gloating. Because I finally had *that* dog. The one who would stick to my side. Who sat calmly and listened to what I had to say. But what I didn't take into account was Thorp's weakness—his attachment to me and his desire to please me—which would not allow him to leave my side for certain commands. He also wasn't very food motivated. All he wanted was to sit on my lap and be loved. His confidence was fragile—he didn't have that ambition most dogs have. He was, after all, a mill dog, so training Thorp had its own challenges.

After filling out all of the required paperwork and paying the testing fees, it was time to take the Therapy Dogs International and the Canine Good Citizen tests, conducted simultaneously.

The evaluator was so nice, so calm and so kind. She eased my anxiety, and we began the testing. She touched Thorp all over, and brushed him. She had me walk by another dog and by some children. We walked up to a person pretending to be disabled in a wheelchair. We took a stroll by a person walking with crutches. Thorp did everything perfectly.

But the moment of truth was yet to come. The down command and the sit-stay: it was time. I walked him over to the evaluator, my heart racing, and I told Thorp to sit. I took a deep breath and said, "Down, Thorp," as I pointed to the ground . . . He looked up at me, and he lay down as though it were never a big deal.

A weight was lifted from my shoulders, and my heartbeat slowed. Still one more test: the sit-stay.

I had him get up from the down command and told him to sit and stay. I cautiously walked back fifty feet, the required distance. I felt like I was holding my breath, praying and sweating all at the same time. It was as though the whole room were moving in slow motion. All I could think was, "Please stay. Thorp, stay."

Before I knew it, even though it seemed like forever, the evaluator said, "You can return to your dog."

Return? My head was spinning . . . that meant he really did stay. Thorp did it. He did it!

Then the evaluator said, "OK, put your dog in a sit-stay and walk half the distance away."

"Huh? I don't remember that part of the test," I thought to myself.

I put Thorp in the sit-stay, praying again that he could pull it off, and I walked twenty-five feet away.

The evaluator said, "Call your dog to come to you."

I said, "Thorp, come."

He just sat there, looking at me. We hadn't practiced this—we had practiced staying, and I could see in his eyes that he was confused, unsure. This command was against everything that he was taught, everything he was made to practice every day for the last two weeks.

Coming to me, at this moment, meant not obeying. My heart skipped a beat, and I said, "Thorpy, it's OK, come."

It was as though Lassie was running home or Chance from *Homeward Bound* was making his way up the hill . . . Thorp was coming to me—and it meant Thorp had passed the test!

He did it—we did it. From living in a chicken-wire cage two years ago to becoming a certified therapy dog. The two of us had come a long way—a very long way.

The tears of anguish I had shed while carrying Thorp out of a barn were now tears of pure elation. I felt like Thorp knew how important this was to me, as I knew it was to him.

This was all part of the plan that neither of us had in mind that cold day on March 12, 2008.

Thorp sat next to me, proud as could be as Susan snapped our picture, and I glowed, holding our passing test. A much different photo than two years earlier.

CHAPTER 45

LOOKING FOR WORK

Nothing came easily for Thorp or me. Once we obtained the official certification papers, Thorp and I hit the pavement, looking for jobs. Amazingly, no one wanted us. The library said that their "Read to the Dog" program was unsuccessful. This program had therapy dogs come to a library or school and allowed children to read to them. (It is thought that therapy animals give children confidence to read because they don't correct or interrupt them.) Our school district took down our information but never called back.

It was disheartening. All of the struggle we had both faced—the mountains we had climbed, and here we were at what seemed like the top, yet it still felt so empty.

Months would pass before a fated meeting would take place. Like all opportunities fate provides, Thorp and I would find ourselves in a place previously unimaginable.

My parents were in town for Christmas, and their friends from Florida were also in town, visiting their daughter. We all went to dinner, and Mary and I started talking. She was a teacher at a special education school in my district for children with emotional and behavioral disorders. Her work inspired me, but I failed to make the connection that night.

Days later, I texted her and asked if she would be interested in having Thorp come to her classroom and be with the kids. She was thrilled. I met with the principal, and in a few weeks, with all of the paperwork submitted, Thorp and I walked into Clay Academy—a place in which we had never seen ourselves.

The work we do at Clay is unlike any work I have done. Working with kids was never my calling, but with Thorp at my side, being with the kids has become one of the most fulfilling experiences of my life.

But even better is how the kids react to Thorp. The students' disabilities range from severe autism to mental illness. They are unable to be served in their own school districts, so they attend Clay Academy. Many of the children come from difficult family situations, and all of them are challenged by their disabilities to the point of not being able to function in a mainstream classroom.

But when Thorp entered the room on the very first day, it was as though I could feel the world open up and become brighter, lighter. One of the boys who processes things as if he were four years of age, ran to Thorp and put his arms around him. While it was hard to understand what he was saying, it was not hard to see the smile on his face.

Thorp is a mainstay in the classroom. The students count on us to be there. They take Thorp for walks, they talk to him, and they read to him. Most important of all, they can just be with him. There are times when the social worker uses Thorp to break through to a student in crisis.

Once, there was a young girl who suffered from mental illness and the long-term effects of physical abuse. It was hard for her to cope in the classroom, especially during conflict. She had a difficult time expressing herself and caused a lot of disruption. The social worker took her out of the classroom and asked Thorp to join her. We started slowly. Thorp and I just sat in the room. I didn't talk; it wasn't my place to say anything, but it is a regulation that the handler be with the dog at all times.

The social worker began her session, and she remained frozen. I let Thorp's leash go, and he stepped toward her. She hesitated, but after a few moments reached her hand toward Thorp, and he met it. She stroked his head and slowly began to speak.

He gave her enough comfort to allow her to feel strength. Dogs empower people simply by offering unconditional love and silent compassion.

Through everything the kids throw at him and all the situations that present themselves, Thorp sits quietly. Always gentle, he lies with the kids on our reading blanket, and I believe that he takes it all in. I take it all in.

Never would I have pictured myself working with emotionally challenged kids. But I am there, teaching them, reading with them, talking with them. They ask where Thorp came from, and I tell them. I tell them of his struggles, and they can relate to Thorp. They understand what it is like to be scared, to not trust, and to be misunderstood.

I believe that they can see Thorp's soul.

It is not just the younger kids. At Clay, there are high school students, and while Thorp and I don't work directly with them, we come in contact with them when we are there. There was a young man who struggled with authority and often acted out violently, but he always came to Thorp with his hand stretched out, so gentle and kind. If only for one brief moment, it was as though that boy had no worries in the world.

A girl who struggled with fitting in and staying out of trouble would whisper to Thorp and reach out her hand to pet him when she thought no one was looking. The amazing part is that Thorp always walks to them. It is as though he can sense their need for him. And maybe, because Thorp knows what it is like to feel alone, he understands that he needs to be there for them.

Thorp might not understand their disabilities—instead, he sees beyond them, and the kids feel free to be who they are with Thorp.

Working at Clay has changed both our lives and the lives of dozens of kids who now believe that they have this furry guy on their side. Someone they can read to without judgment, someone they can snuggle when they are having a hard day, and someone they can play and have fun with.

CHAPTER 46

FINALLY HEARD

In February 2012, I went to Antarctica for three weeks, and Mary made my trip an entire learning experience for the students. We had them draw and color a "flat Thorp" for me to bring along and take pictures with, and when I returned, we spent time going through my photos. My trip became their trip, and our common traveler was Thorp.

It was such a success that the *Northwest Herald* came to the school to do a piece on it. And when I least expected it, the reporter asked about Thorp. I explained his background and what I had done to save him, and the real details of the Wisconsin puppy mills were finally printed.

Thorp's history was officially meshed with his future, and it was for all the world to read.

The article still didn't include anything about pet stores. That piece of the issue remains to be reported in the *Northwest Herald*. I haven't given up.

Regardless of the battles we have yet to win, Thorp and I are proud of the voice we found together.

The one we used to tell the truth we both knew existed, a truth so few believed.

We both look towards a future without puppy mills and pet stores while continuing to share our story and reminding others of the gruesome tragedy of the mills.

I could have saved any one of the dogs that day in March—but I saved Thorp, and that has made all of the difference.

AFTERWORD

As of this book's publication, approximately 10,000 puppy mills still exist throughout the United States. While auctions are now illegal in Wisconsin, they are still prevalent in many other states. Hundreds of dogs are bought and sold weekly just like they were in Clark County.

Sadly, places like Petland still exist—even in my county. Approximately, half of the states have passed stronger laws to regulate puppy mills, and federal legislation has extended regulations to online purchasing. Many larger cities across the States have passed ordinances to prevent pet stores from selling dogs, cats and rabbits unless they are from a rescue. But millions of puppies from mills are still sold to unknowing consumers, and thousands of dogs sit in metal crates—never to see the light of day or to feel the touch of a gentle human hand.

The puppy-mill fight is far from over, as many states refuse to end or even regulate the horrid business.

My hope is that, like me, you will want to do something to make a difference. It would be easy to close the book and hope things change, but it takes ALL of our voices to make a difference.

If you question your strength or hesitate because you are unsure of what you could possibly do, please remember Thorp, Mully and Penelope were freed regardless of my own insecurities, my own shortcomings and my lack of experience. I chose to jump in and to act. You can, too!

It is up to all of us to speak for the dogs who have no voice.

WAYS TO HELP

- <u>Share this story.</u> Help educate others on what puppy mils are and where puppies in pet stores and on-line come from.

- <u>Volunteer at a shelter or rescue.</u> There are many opportunities: walking dogs, socializing cats, cleaning kennels, coordinating adoptions, providing transport, photographing adoptable pets, creating/managing websites and blogs. The possibilities are endless. And please consider fostering a pet in your home. For each pet fostered, there is space for a homeless pet in a shelter. Fostering saves lives.

- <u>Contact legislators</u> and let them know animal-welfare legislation is important to you. If you can provide them with a specific bill currently up for vote, all the better.

- DON'T shop at a pet store where puppies are sold.

- ADOPT your next pet!

- <u>Have faith</u> that as a united front, all of us can change the world for animals.

For more information on getting involved and resources for adopting a pet, please visit:
www.beckymonroe.com.

ACKNOWLEDGMENTS

This journey has been amazing. From heart-wrenching experiences to moments of pure joy, I certainly learned I have many people to appreciate and thank for helping me survive such a pivotal transformation.

To Bill and Abby: No words could convey how grateful I am for your support. You never questioned my beliefs or tried to hold me back, even though there were definitely times I seemed crazy and emotionally drained. You learned to live among an ark of animals. You allowed me to follow my heart, even if it meant letting me go or seeing me in pain. Because of your understanding, I followed my passion and found peace. Thank you.

To Susan, Bill and Margie: Thank you for taking part in my journey. For attending the auctions and for being friends who truly understand what I saw. You share in my vision to end the atrocity and have always believed in my actions.

To Ellen: You taught me from our first days at animal control how to be strong and to fight for the animals. You always knew this path was painful for me, but you never told me to stop or allowed me to walk away. You believed in my story and knew how important it was for me to tell.

To Delreen: Our friendship keeps me alive. There were many days when just knowing you understood my pain made it all hurt less. Our daily e-mails gave me more strength than you will ever know and always gave me the courage to keep fighting.

To Kelly: My lifelong, dearest friend . . . Not only have you always been at my side, caring for creatures, you have always encouraged me to follow my passion. When I almost gave up on this book, you pushed me to realize its importance and offered your expertise and encouragement to finally get it done. Thank you.

To Frank: Thank you for reviewing my book and for providing your insight. Unknowingly, we walked side by side through the trenches of the puppy-mill movement in Wisconsin. You were and will always be a pioneer for the animals. You go where no man has gone before, and I am blessed to know you.

To Shayla and all of the Wisconsin Rescue Platform: Thank you for accepting me into the group and for allowing a novice rescuer to be part of something so spectacular.

To Chuck: Thank you for sharing your amazing story, "The Box." But, more important, for all you and Sherry do every day at Clark County Humane. Your work there is miraculous. Thousands of dogs have homes because of your dedication.

Animal- welfare laws in Wisconsin are better because you never gave up.

To Carol: Where would I be if we hadn't become friends that horrible day in March? Thank you for taking me in and teaching me. Thank you for guiding me when I felt helpless. You have always been a mentor and a pillar of strength for me on this journey. And thank you for allowing me to include your training guide for puppy-mill dogs. It is a great resource.

To Marcia: So many said that the story was too sad, too tragic, but you taught me that people are stronger than publishers give readers credit for. You always had faith in my message. Thank you for preserving my voice and my story as you took your "pen" to my manuscript. You turned it into something I could proudly publish!

Tips on Fostering Puppy-Mill Dogs
By Carol Sumbry

I have several favorite sayings about fostering dogs from puppy mills. First, to paraphrase the U.S. Army slogan, I want them to "be all they can be," meaning that just because they have lived their whole life in cages, we shouldn't set limits on them. Some can go on to be therapy dogs. Some will be very well-adjusted. Some will always be shy. My job in giving them a foster home is to show them there is more to life and take them as far as they can go.

Another saying is that it's my job to put as much as I can "on their resume." For example, one mill dog may always be shy or afraid of men, but if I can work really hard on everything else, then she becomes more adoptable. Therefore, I work hard on manners, crate training, commands, housetraining, and so on. The more this dog has on her "resume," the more likely an adopter will overlook a little shyness or fear of certain things. I'll be able to say, "Yes, this dog is shy, but she knows how to sit . . . is perfect in a crate . . . rides well in the car . . . walks great on leash . . ." You get the idea!

I have fostered quite a few mill dogs over the years. Some have gone on to lead normal, well-adjusted lives just like any other dog. A few have gone to humane education events with me. All have learned to enjoy walks. A few carry a lot of the "wounds" or fears from the mill, but in providing a foster home, you have to give them every opportunity to lead a normal life. Merely feeling sorry for them doesn't help. This reminds me of another favorite saying: "You can heal the wounds, but the scars often remain forever." We can't always fix everything, but at least we can try to fix what we can.

A friend told me another great saying: "Look back, but don't stare." This means it's good to know where these dogs have come from and what they have had to endure, but both they and we have to move on. Sometimes we overanalyze everything they do or question why they do it, but we'll never understand in their terms exactly what it was like to live as a dog in a mill. Also, any mill dog in our care represents one of the lucky ones that got out. So many never do!

A few things I have learned about mill dogs along the way
By Carol Sumbry

Pairs   Most puppy-mill dogs have been raised in a pack and in fact were never alone, so they enjoy other dogs and find comfort in being with them. Many have difficulty living as an only dog. Even though they need to bond with people and I do separate them from the pack, still they thrive in a pack.

Puppy mentality   Since a mill dog has had limited experiences in life, everything outside the mill is a whole new world to him. Adopting an adult mill dog is almost like adopting a puppy. We must introduce changes slowly and positively.

Use a long line   For the dog's safety and your peace of mind, keep her on a long leash at all times (except when she's unattended in a secure location indoors). A frightened dog often tries to run away, but chasing her only makes her more fearful. Instead, when she bolts, you can easily catch her by stepping on the leash as she goes by. Don't drag her toward you. Simply use the leash to keep her in place while you approach slowly. Using this technique, you can eventually teach her to wait or freeze when startled.

Fences   Check that all fencing is secure. Also, *every* mill dog should initially be on a long line, *even when outdoors,* until the dog can be trusted to wait or freeze. These dogs aren't used to huge open spaces, and once they're outside in a fenced yard, they may panic and run or even climb a fence to get away.

Crate   Make sure your puppy-mill dog has a crate. So often we hear: "But he spent his whole life in a crate, so I don't want to do that." Yet a crate can provide comfort and security to a mill dog. Also, since he's never experienced a home environment, a crate is essential for his safety. He hasn't learned not to dash out the door. Safety first! The crate also makes it easier to teach him to mind his manners (no rooting through the trash can) as well as to become housetrained, so it helps make adoption easier.

Feeding Feed the dog in her crate. Living in a mill cage makes some dogs aggressive over food, while others were afraid to eat and never got enough. Feeding in a secure place like a crate eliminates any competition at mealtime. This practice also encourages clean crate habits. Many mill dogs are afraid of bowls/food, as mealtime was the only time the "miller" came around.

Safety-proof your house Mill dogs don't know about stairs, so secure the area above each stairway to prevent falls. They don't understand furniture or heights, so don't allow them to jump on and off the furniture and hurt themselves. Secure trash cans and other temptations in the environment, much as you would for the safety of a puppy or toddler. Remember, this is a whole new world.

Beware of going off leash So often we hear people say: "But I know my dog, and he's fine"—often after just weeks in the foster home. Don't be lulled into a false sense of security because your dog seems to stay nearby or isn't frightened during the first few weeks. Some dogs are almost in "culture shock" with all the new smells, sounds, and sights in their world. As they adjust, it can take months or even a year to see their full temperament and reactions to the environment. Has your dog heard an ambulance go by? The crash of thunder? The tornado-warning siren? Your dog hasn't experienced a lot in the first few weeks, so beware of a false sense of security from the initial "shocked" period of no reaction.

Housetraining   Most info on mill dogs will tell you how hard they are to housetrain. I disagree. This is not difficult *if* handled correctly and, again, slowly. My experience is that most mill dogs found a place in their teeny pen where they tried to keep clean, and they will carry that over. By using a crate and introducing your mill dog to the rest of the house slowly, room by room, you can teach her to keep her new larger den (your home) clean. Treat your new dog as if she's a puppy, and with reward, praise, patience and consistency, housetraining can be successful. If your dog is very small, you may want to consider indoor training. I suggest picking one or the other (indoor or outdoor) and sticking with it.

Flight risk   All puppy-mill survivors are high flight risks. Never take your dog outside a securely fenced yard until you are thoroughly bonded. Then, if you take your dog outside the fence, double-check to be sure his harness is secure. I sometimes use a collar and harness, then run the lead from the collar through the harness for extra safety. If a mill dog gets loose outside a secured area, he will likely run until he drops; catching him will be quite a feat. Prevention is by far the best policy.

Doorways   Many mill dogs are quite fearful of passing a person while going through an open door. Many will *run* through doors. You must open the door wide and stand behind it so that your dog feels safe. You might even need to stand a distance beyond the open door to get her to follow. Also, when frightened, your dog may unexpectedly dash out the front door; so if your yard isn't fenced, it's a good idea to put up baby gates at all exterior doors that the dog might be able to reach.

Coprophagy   Stool-eating is common in puppy-mill survivors. While there is much contention as to the cause, most rescuers feel it is a learned behavior. Again, prevention is the best policy.

Clean up the yard frequently. Some mill dogs stop this behavior over time.

Heath issues   Many mill dogs are prone to dental problems due to poor diet and lack of care when younger. If you have ever had a toothache, you know how painful this can be. As part of your commitment to rescuing a mill dog, make sure he gets the comfort he deserves through proper dental care via your vet. Also, because mill dogs usually live in damp housing, a soft warm place as they age is a must for sore joints. Dietary supplements like MSM and glucosamine can also help ease sore joints as mill dogs age.

Leash training   Many mill dogs have lived on chicken wire, so grass and even solid ground are new to them. They have also never pottied while on leash, so learning this can take time. Leash training should be gradual and gentle. Never pull a dog by the leash, as this is reminiscent of being grabbed by the neck—a common puppy-mill practice.

Collar/harness   Many mill dogs respond more positively to a well-fitted harness. Whether you choose collar or harness, make sure it is secure. When truly frightened, mill dogs can buck out of either—*and if a mill dog gets loose, he may never be caught again!* Collars must be tight. It's recommended that you initially use *both* a collar *and* a harness for safety, so that if the dog slips out of one, the other is still attached. Usually, two leashes or a "coupler" attached to a leash/harness works fine for this double safety technique.

ID   Make sure your dog is always wearing an ID tag!

Touching/picking up the dog   Try massage/TTouch. Keep it short and positive. Resist the urge to pick up your mill dog, especially at first. Many mill dogs just don't enjoy being picked up, and so I try to separate out handling and picking up; in other words, I teach them first that "hands are good" through gentle petting, massage and TTouch, without picking up the dog. Do not touch or pet around the head or neck initially, as most mill dogs are not comfortable with this type of petting. Most have never been held or were only held and picked up for negative experiences. If you must pick up your dog, make sure he can see you picking him up. It's good to put a word to it prior to picking up the dog, such as saying "up" in a cheerful tone. Hold the dog securely while gently stroking his back. Some dogs never learn to feel safe or enjoy being picked up due to their mill treatment.

Attention The dog's whole life up to this point has been built around survival only. It's your job to keep him safe and secure while he learns about life and love. Yes, there's a lot to make up for, but a little bit of love at a time works best. Dogs live in the moment, so you can't go back and "make up" for what they didn't have. Mill dogs have had nothing, and therefore they may attach to you quickly. If you give them too much too soon, they'll find it difficult to adjust when you have to take it away later. For example, don't take weeks off work and spend every minute with the dog. You are only setting her up for disaster when you later return to a normal routine. Get her used to what her new world will be like. She still needs to spend time alone in a crate. She must learn to deal with life beyond you, so introduce love, attention and her new world slowly.

Confidence Dogs that learn new things become more confident. A puppy-mill dog will have more confidence if you can teach commands like "wait" and "touch"—my two favorites for mill dogs.

Fitted clothing to reduce stress A close-fitting T-shirt purchased at a pet store or made from a toddler's T-shirt or tank can help reduce the dog's anxiety. You can also purchase an anxiety wrap, which uses a technique called maintained pressure to calm your animal by soothing the sensory receptors. It is similar to swaddling a baby or using a "hug box" to calm autistic children. Though it sounds a little "out there," the connection between sensory stimuli and behavioral patterns has long been a staple of such touch therapies as Tellington TTouch. For more information, see www.anxietywrap.com.

Routine   All dogs prefer routine, but puppy-mill dogs thrive on routine. They like to know what's coming next. Don't change too many things in a dog's world at once. A predictable routine will help him adjust to living outside the four walls of the mill.

Journaling   It can be helpful to keep a journal on the progress of your puppy-mill dog, even if you only write entries once a week. Rehabbing the puppy-mill dog can be frustrating at times. Often, progress occurs in baby steps. A journal will help you look back and chart how far your dog has come. Sometimes we forget what wonderful strides we have made on the journey if we don't look back to where we started.

I believe that once our lives have been changed by a mill dog, we're responsible to those left behind. We must use our knowledge to educate others and speak for those who have no voice. Only through education can we change the lives of our furry friends imprisoned in the mills.

Someone with a three-legged mill dog once told me they were unsure how to answer questions and were a little embarrassed to discuss their dog's previous life. I believe that anyone who has helped save one of these precious creatures should be proud. That person is a hero and shouldn't be afraid to share the stories!

It is imperative for us to speak for those who can't speak for themselves. We must educate people and change the laws for those dogs that are left behind.

Puppy-mill dogs are innocent victims in a world run by greed! Adopting and rehabilitating them takes time, love and patience, but the rewards are tenfold. These dogs can blossom into wonderful companions that will be grateful for a chance to experience life outside the mill.